CHILD LIFE
COOK BOOK

By

CLARA INGRAM JUDSON

Author of "Cooking Without Mother's Help," "Junior
Cook Book," "Sewing Without Mother's Help," "Billy
Robin and His Neighbors," "Jerry and Jean, Detec-
tors," "Flower Fairies," "Foxy Squirrel in the Garden,"
"Garden Adventures in Winter," etc.

RAND McNALLY & COMPANY
NEW YORK   CHICAGO   SAN FRANCISCO

PRYOR PUBLICATIONS
WHITSTABLE AND WYRLEY

Specialist in Facsimile Reproductions

MEMBER OF
INDEPENDENT PUBLISHERS GUILD

75 Dargate Road, Yorkletts, Whitstable,
Kent CT5 3AE, England
Tel. & Fax: (01227) 274655

E-mail: alan@pryor-publications.co.uk

www.pryor-publications.co.uk

Kent Exporter of the Year Awards Winner 1998/2000

First Published by Rand McNally in 1926.

This Facsimile Edition Published in May 2003
By Pryor Publications

I SBN 0 –946014-73-6

A full list of Titles sent free on request

Printed and Bound in Great Britain

To

Every Girl and Boy

Who Enjoys Cooking

THE INTRODUCTION

This introduction is for GROWN-UPS.   Boys and girls may skip it and begin with page 1.

SCENES IN TWO KITCHENS

The first kitchen:

"Mother, please may I try to make some cookies?"   Margaret's eyes were shining eagerly as she waited for her mother's reply.

"Oh, you don't really know how, Margaret, and the cookies wouldn't be fit for anyone to eat.   The materials would only be wasted.   Besides, I would have to do most of the work, and I'm busy today.   I just can't have you messing up my clean kitchen."   She hurried into the pantry without seeing the disappointed look on her small daughter's face.

The second kitchen:

"Oh, Jack!" called Sallie to her brother in the back yard.   "Mother says we may have the kitchen this afternoon.   I'm going to make some cookies.   Want to help?"

"You bet!" shouted Jack, rushing in and slamming the door behind him.   "Where are the nuts?   And how about chopping up some dates?"

Soon both children were happily at work with big aprons tied about them, and newspapers spread out on the floor.

It would not be difficult to decide which were the happier children in these two homes. One cannot help wishing that all mothers might display the wisdom shown by Sallie's mother.

CHILD LIFE COOK BOOK has been prepared by Mrs. Judson for the guidance of children fortunate enough to have homes like that of Jack and Sallie.   With its help girls and boys may engage in the fascinating activity of cooking without the aid of adults, and with economy and precision in the use of materials and with assurance of success in their efforts.

There are two things which determine the value of a certain activity for children.   Can it engage and hold their interest?   Will its mastery still be useful when the boys and girls are no longer children?

The pleasure shown by children when permitted to experiment in the kitchen proves that the activity of cooking quickly engages and holds their interest.   The universal need for care in the choice and preparation of food is proof of the usefulness of this activity. Is it not a safe assumption that the little girl who has such happy experiences as those of Sallie will in later years be alert to maintain the health and comfort of her family with a fine economy of money and effort?   Will she not be able to invest the routine of meal getting with dignity and charm?

Educational activities of sound value are incorporated in the entire series of THE RAND McNALLY ACTIVITIES BOOKS, of which this volume is a part.   These books are planned to satisfy and stimulate the natural creative impulses of boys and girls. Under their guidance the experiences suggested are made fruitful and of permanent worth.

In THE CHILD LIFE COOK BOOK such ends are attained through the fortunate combination of the author's practical knowledge of the subject and a genuine understanding of the interests of children.

MIRIAM BLANTON HUBER

APPLES

DO YOU like to cook? You say you never tried? Think of that—and cooking is such fun, too! A person just feels sorry for a girl or boy who is old enough to read this book and who really doesn't know how to cook anything.

You notice I said boy just as surely as I said girl. For how in the world is a boy going to manage a camping trip or even a one-day picnic in the woods if he doesn't know how to cook? It doesn't matter where you live, in a big city, or a nice comfortable town, or the beautiful wide country, everyone who eats should learn how to cook— that's just plain good sense. It's fun, too.

Do you want to know a secret? All right, here it is! Girls and boys who start cooking from this cook book right now, and do all the cooking they possibly can, will be ready for cooking a whole meal very soon. But you have to pay attention to every direction, and obey orders, and practice in your own kitchen— if you want to be a good cook.

* * * * * * * * *

Now what do you suppose happened right between this sentence and the one before the stars? Tom put the book down and sighed a big sigh and Nellie said, "There now! I told you anything so lovely wouldn't work. Mother doesn't like us to mess up the kitchen!"

When here, if they had only read a little, just a wee little more, they'd have found all about *that*.

Of course Mother may not like you to "mess up the kitchen." Would you like her to come into your room and turn things upside down so you couldn't find a thing? Why you don't even like cleaning day very well because your things get put around other places from where you've had them. And cleaning day never gets your things messy as you sometimes do the kitchen. Nobody, not even Mother, likes to have a workshop mussed up, and the kitchen is Mother's workshop.

But if you read *all* the cooking lesson every time, and do everything it says to do, you'll leave the kitchen just as orderly and clean as you found it and first thing you know, Mother will be saying, "Won't you please cook us something good again today?"

Now to begin. Find a corner in a drawer or on a shelf that you can have for your cooking things. Then get a towel, a bar of hand soap, a little wooden stick for cleaning finger nails, and an apron. Remember that every time, after you have done your cooking lesson, the towel must be put in the wash or it must be thoroughly dried and folded up and put away. All the supplies must be put away in order after each cooking lesson. Then they'll be ready for next time.

Every time, before you start to cook, give your hands a very careful washing, rinse the soap off and dry them well. Clean your nails with the little wooden stick, put on your apron and you are ready to be Mr. or Miss Cook.

Notice that the recipe is printed in two kinds of type. The black type is the real recipe; the lighter type tells about the recipe so you will be sure to

understand exactly what to do in every step of the way. Be sure to read the whole thing through—both kinds of type—before you begin. If there is anything you do not quite understand, read it again so you do. Then, when you begin cooking, do each step exactly as the rule says and you will find it very simple and easy to get a good result.

For our first lesson we will cook something that can be enjoyed at any meal—breakfast, luncheon or supper, and dinner. After you have learned to cook baked apples easily, cook apples by the other recipes until you are "apple perfect." That means, until you are sure you can cook apples in several delicious ways. Then you will be ready to begin at the beginning of a whole meal and learn your way right through the menu. Isn't that going to be fun?

The recipe is for four people. If there are more (or less) in your family, you can make the recipe bigger or smaller as needed. We're going to cook something everyone likes to eat.

BAKED APPLES

Get out four fine apples, the box of sugar, an apple corer, a tablespoon, a teaspoon, a baking dish, the box of ground cinnamon, a pat of butter and measure out a cupful of water. Arrange all these things conveniently on the table. Now is the time to light the oven. If you are not allowed to do this, ask some one to please do it for you. If you cook with a coal oven, see that the dampers are set.

With a bit of clean tissue paper, butter the bottom of the baking dish.

Wash the apples and wipe dry.

Core the apples, and place them upright in the baking dish. (To core an apple, push the corer straight through the apple in the center, turn the corer and then pull it back out. It will bring the core with it. Don't save the core.)

Fill the core-holes with sugar—just as full as they will hold.

Put ½ teaspoonful butter over each hole.

Sprinkle ¼ teaspoonful ground cinnamon over each apple.

Pour the cupful of water into the dish.

Set the dish of apples into the oven.

Bake for one hour. See that the oven does not get too hot; your apples must keep nice and brown but not scorch.

Look into the oven every 15 minutes to make sure they are not cooking too fast.

Serve in individual dishes with cream and sugar.

* * * * * * * * *

While the apples are baking, wash the corer, spoons and cup and put them away. Put away all your supplies where you found them. Wipe off the kitchen table and brush up the floor.

After the apples are taken from the baking dish, fill the dish with cold water and let it soak until after dinner when you can slip out and wash it.

Now answer truly—*did* you ever eat such good baked apples as yours?

APPLE SAUCE

Wash, peel, cut in eighths and remove cores from enough apples to make four cupfuls. For this you will need about five apples, probably. You may pile the cups when you measure as such large pieces of apples do not pack down into the cup for accurate measurement. While you are peeling and cutting the apples, drop the pieces into a pan of cold water so that the fruit does not turn brown. Use tart cooking apples.

Drain, put into a saucepan and pour over 2 cupfuls of boiling water.

Cover tightly and cook gently until the apples are soft and mushy. This will take about 20 minutes, perhaps a bit less.

Stir gently to be sure the apples are all broken up and soft. Add 1 cupful of granulated sugar. Stir in well.

Cook slowly for 15 minutes. Stir twice during this time to make sure the sauce does not settle to the bottom of the pan and burn. Cook uncovered after the sugar is added.

Remove to a serving dish and serve either hot or cold.

In the late spring, when apples are apt to taste a little "flat," some people like to add 1 tablespoonful of lemon juice, or ½ teaspoonful of nutmeg or ½ teaspoonful ground cinnamon five minutes before the sauce is done. Stir this in well with the last stirring. These seasonings are especially nice if the sauce is to be served cold. Also they make variety.

Apple sauce is often served as a relish with pork—it is tasty and appetizing with both roast pork and chops and aids digestion.

SOUPS—FOR DINNERS

NOW that you have learned to cook apples so well, you are ready to begin work on the meal we promised you should learn to cook.

Any well organized meal begins with soup—hot and tasty. That doesn't mean that you *must* have soup at every single luncheon or dinner! My no! How tiresome that would be! But it does mean that *mostly* we have soup at dinner because it makes us feel rested and comfortable before we begin on the main course. And sometimes we have it for luncheon, too, just because it is so good.

Soup is such an important form of food that we shall have two lessons for it. This first lesson will be mostly on soups that are good for a dinner. The next lesson will be mostly soups that have a protein value (that means, can be used in place of meat), and so are especially good for a luncheon or supper meal. But any of the soups we shall learn are good for either meal if you want to use your favorites for both times.

Perhaps it would be interesting to stop right here and talk a few minutes about the different meals of the day and why we have them so. We have three meals and they are just as different as three meals can be, aren't they? Of course, because during the day we need different sorts of food and we have varying lengths of time to spend in eating our meals.

In the morning everyone wants some fruit and something warm and nourishing to start the day right. And few people plan so that they have much time for leisurely eating, unless perhaps Sunday morning, which is different from a work-a-day time. So we eat fruit and cereal and maybe toast and eggs or muffins and bacon. And we drink some hot beverage. Grown folks usually choose coffee, and children cocoa in winter and just plain milk the rest of the year. No well brought up child drinks coffee

these days we are glad to know! If we are late, we take our fruit and cereal and milk and eat it slowly, knowing that is the best sort of a breakfast. It is much better to eat just that much and stop than to rush and eat more without careful chewing. That seems odd, but it is true. Time for chewing is so very important.

For luncheon we want a hot soup—the kind we will study next lesson maybe—or potatoes with cheese, or fish, or a nut dish, or something that has some meat value, and with that we take at least one vegetable and either fresh fruit or a fresh green vegetable. The dessert, if we have one (it isn't really necessary if the rest of the luncheon is ample and nourishing) is simpler than a dessert for dinner would be. Maybe we choose gelatine, or gingerbread, or boiled apples, or a plain custard. The kind of dessert we have, if we have any, depends on the sort of luncheon that came *before* dessert, you see, so that the meal as a whole is just enough, but not too much.

Sometimes one has dinner at noon. Some people have noon dinner all the time, some have it only on Sunday. Wherever it is possible evening dinner is fine, except for very young children, because in the evening there is more leisure for eating and for jolly talk at the table. The day's work is done and everyone has time to be comfortable and sociable. But if you have dinner at noon, your luncheon meal appears in the evening with the name of "supper" attached to it. Don't let a change of name fool you! It is just the same sort of meal as a luncheon, only eaten at the different time of day.

For dinner we have three or four courses, instead of the two we usually have for luncheon or supper. We have a soup. Then a meat dish with two vegetables and bread and maybe some relishes. Then a salad with a bit of a wafer. Then a dessert.

That's when it is four courses. When dinner is three courses we usually leave off the dessert; it's apt to be rich and we don't want to eat too much of that kind of food. So we skip dessert sometimes. In hot weather we sometimes skip soup, or maybe we have fruit, iced until it is cold and delicious, in the place of soup. Then sometimes we have only one vegetable and serve a plain lettuce salad with the meat course. Or we can have celery and radishes as a relish and skip the salad course entirely once in a while.

You see, the interesting thing about cooking and planning meals is that it never need get tiresome—there is *always* some new combination to plan, if only we think hard and find it.

Now we are going to begin with a dinner and this lesson is on the first course. We are going to make Cream of Spinach Soup. And we are counting on serving four. If you have more, or less, in your family, change the recipe to suit.

CREAM OF SPINACH SOUP

Get out a double boiler, a measuring cup, 3 cupfuls of milk, 1 cupful of cooked spinach, some butter, salt, flour, a wire sieve and a cooking spoon. Arrange them conveniently on the table.

Put 1 pint of water in the lower part of the double boiler and set it to heat. (On the inside of the cover you'll see how many cups make a pint.)

While the water is getting hot, rub the spinach through the wire sieve (use the cooking spoon.)

Put 2¾ cupfuls of milk and the strained spinach in the upper part of the boiler and set it to heat.

Mix 2 teaspoonfuls of flour with the ¼ cupful of milk. Mix until there isn't a lump to be found. Then stir in 1 teaspoonful of salt.

Now stir the milk and spinach with your big spoon and see that they are getting steaming hot.

Drop 2 tablespoonfuls of butter into the milk and spinach.

When the butter has melted and the milk is steaming, stir in your flour and salt mixture. Stir well for two minutes.

Cover and let cook for ten minutes.

While the soup is cooking, wash the sieve, cup and small spoon and put the clean tools and the supplies away.

Serve the soup on warmed soup plates. If you want it to be very dressy, sprinkle freshly popped corn over each plate of soup just before you take it into the dining room. This will look pretty, and taste fine.

After you have taken up the soup, quickly fill the boiler with cold water. After luncheon you can easily wash it.

All this may take an hour, so start in time. If you get the soup ready ahead of time, pull the boiler back where the soup will keep hot but will not cook. A little waiting will not spoil it.

CREAM OF CELERY SOUP

Wash and clean carefully the coarse, outside pieces and the roots of 2 stalks of celery. Drop the tender inside pieces into cold water and set aside to crisp. Serve these as a relish with the soup.

Dice the coarse stalks and roots very fine. There should be at least 1 cupful, pressed down tightly. If you have more, so much the better.

Cover with 2 cupfuls of boiling water and simmer for 35 minutes. If you ever want to make this soup in a shorter time than 45 minutes, you can cook the celery at a brisk boil for 15 minutes. But the longer, slower cooking makes a slightly better flavor and takes no more gas because of the lower flame needed.

Cook tightly covered.

By this time half the water has boiled away.

Add 3 cupfuls of milk
    1 tablespoonful butter
    1 teaspoonful salt.

Serve at once with hot toasted crackers.

CLEAR TOMATO SOUP

To one cupful of tomato extract add
    3 cupfuls of boiling water
    1 teaspoonful salt
    1 tablespoonful chopped parsley.

Bring to a boil and serve at once.

Tomato extract—sometimes called tomato essence or tomato pulp—can be purchased in small cans holding about one cupful each. Hence this is about the very quickest and easiest soup that can possibly be made.

For variety, several different seasonings can be used instead of parsley. For instance, 2 tablespoonfuls of chopped mushrooms; or 1 tablespoonful of chopped sweet pepper; or 1 tablespoonful chopped onion or chives or carrots, or 2 tablespoonfuls chopped spinach. In each case the finished soup tastes quite differently.

SOUPS—FOR LUNCHEON OR SUPPER

THIS lesson is on soups that are especially good for luncheon or supper. That does not mean that they are not also good for dinner—dear me, no! But it does mean that they have more value as nourishment than the soups in the other lesson and you will enjoy these, especially when you have less to eat in the rest of the meal.

The soup we choose first is a kind that will taste best when you come in from a good play in the snow, and is also delicious when the weather is hot in summer. Then, too, it is something that not many cooks know how to make, so listen carefully. You are going to have something both good and unusual —Peanut Butter Soup.

Maybe you will try this first for a Saturday luncheon. So after you have had your morning play, remember to scrub up till hands and face are spotlessly clean, not forgetting the finger nails, a cosy place for dirt if you don't watch closely. By the way, in the winter, a person must be very careful to *dry* hands well after washing. None of this looking at a towel and calling it done, unless you want horrid, rough chaps instead of smooth, clean skin. So take time to dry well, fold the towel neatly on the rack, and tidy the washstand before you say you have finished washing.

Then we shall put on aprons and get out all the utensils and supplies needed. As you get to be more experienced in cooking you will, no doubt, before the morning you mean to cook, read over the whole cooking lesson and ask Mother if she will please order the things you will need. That's the only way to make sure you have everything when you want it. You know good cooks never go dashing off to the grocery at the last minute. "Make your head save your heels" is what Grandmother used to tell us, and it's good advice now.

You will need a double boiler, a measuring cup, a teaspoon, and a stirring spoon. For materials you will need a jar of peanut butter, a quart of milk, a tablespoonful of butter, and salt. Then make sure you have some good salt crackers in the pantry, for you will need those to serve with the soup.

The recipe as given is for four persons. If you want more, take half again for six, or twice for eight, or only a half if you are serving two.

PEANUT BUTTER SOUP

Put a quart of water in the lower part of the boiler and bring it to a boil.

Put 4 heaping teaspoonfuls of peanut butter into the upper part. Usually measurements are given level, but as peanut butter is thick and clumsy to measure, you will find heaping spoonfuls the best to manage.

Add ½ cup of milk and cook 10 minutes. Beat till creamy.

Add another ½ cup milk and cook 5 minutes.

Beat till smooth.

Add 1 tablespoonful butter and 1 level teaspoonful salt.

Add 1 cup milk and cook till smooth. Adding the milk gradually keeps the peanut butter from getting lumpy. Be sure your mixture is smooth and creamy each time before you add more milk.

NAVY BEAN SOUP

Wash 1 cupful of navy beans.

Soak them overnight in 3 cupfuls of cold water.

The next day, add 3 cupfuls of hot water and cook gently till the beans are soft enough to mash. This will take about 2 hours of slow cooking. If cooking is done over a simmer burner, they will need very little watching and very little gas.

When tender, mash the beans through a sieve till you have a smooth, soft pulp.

To this pulp add enough meat stock to make 4

cupfuls. If you have no meat stock, use 1 can of canned bouillon and enough water to make 4 cupfuls.

Add 1 teaspoonful salt.

Bring to a boil. Stir enough to mix well.

Serve at once, using 1 teaspoonful of ketchup on each plateful of soup for a garnish.

SPLIT PEA SOUP

Soak 1 cupful of dried split peas overnight in 3 cupfuls of cold water.

Some time the next day, add 3 cupfuls of water and simmer gently till the peas are soft enough to mash. This will take about an hour—maybe longer, so start in plenty of time. Some peas take longer in cooking than others.

When they are cooked tender, mash them through a sieve till you have a smooth, soft pulp.

To this pulp add enough milk to make 4 cupfuls in all.

Add 3 tablespoonfuls of butter and 1 teaspoonful salt.

Bring to a boil and serve at once. "Bring to a boil" means cook it till it is just ready to begin boiling up from the bottom of the pan but does not yet actually boil.

Serve in soup plates that have been warmed and garnish with toasted bread crumbs or with a few kernels of freshly popped corn.

OYSTER SOUP

Prepare a double boiler as for Peanut Butter Soup.

Into the upper part put 3½ cupfuls milk and ½ teaspoonful salt.

Bring to a scald. That means cook till the milk is boiling hot but does not actually boil.

Into a frying pan or an aluminum saucepan put 3 tablespoonfuls of butter and melt it.

Pick over 1 cupful of oysters (½ pint) and make sure there are no shells in the folds.

Put the oysters into the pan with the butter and cook gently till the oysters have frilled edges. This will take 8 or 10 minutes.

Have the soup plates warm and near at hand.

At the last minute, put the oysters into the milk.

Stir a little till well blended and serve at once with toast or crackers.

CREAM OF LIMA BEAN SOUP

Prepare the double boiler as for Peanut Butter soup.

Put 3 cupfuls of milk and 1 teaspoon salt into the upper part. Bring to a scald.

While this is heating put 2 cupfuls of cooked lima beans and 1 cupful boiling water into a saucepan and cook for 10 minutes.

Put the beans through a sieve to remove the hulls. Be sure to mash all the good center part.

Add the pulp to the milk. (There should be about 1 cupful; if more, that is quite all right.)

Add 2 tablespoonfuls of butter. Stir till blended and serve at once with triangles of toasted rye bread.

CREAM OF ASPARAGUS SOUP

Cook the asparagus just as directed on page 14. Use 18 to 20 large stalks or the equivalent.

Rub the asparagus through a coarse sieve to remove the woody portions.

Put into the top part of a double boiler and add 2 tablespoonfuls of butter and 1 cupful of milk.

Stir till well blended and hot.

Then add 3 cupfuls of milk (this makes 4 in all, you see) and stir till it is boiling hot.

If your family like a thicker cream soup, dissolve 2 teaspoonfuls of flour in ¼ cupful of milk (use part of the 4 cupfuls you already plan to put in the soup—and stir into the soup after the first cupful of milk is steaming hot. Then cook the soup for five minutes after it becomes boiling hot. This is necessary to cook the starch in the flour.

Add ½ teaspoon of salt and serve in cups or soup bowls. Garnish with ½ teaspoonful of toasted bread crumbs sprinkled on each serving.

Maybe Mother will allow you to invite two little friends to come to luncheon. You can make the soup, and Mother or cook can provide the rest of the meal. For such a party you might like this menu:

MENU FOR SATURDAY LUNCHEON
Peanut Butter Soup
Salt Crackers
Macaroni with Cheese   Buttered Carrots
Date Muffins   Jam
Apple Pudding   Hard Sauce

One Cook says she thinks that is perfect, only she hopes her Mother will put lots of cheese in the macaroni. Well, of course, that's what we meant, and if you pass the suggestion along with the menu, that is what you will get, we're sure.

MEATS

WE must not linger too long over soups, interesting as it would be to see how many kinds we could learn to make. But we'll do that some other time. Now we want to get on with our dinner.

After soup comes—? The meat course, to be sure. And a very popular course it is, too. Almost everyone likes meat. If it is well cooked, it is a very delicious food, and if it is eaten in moderation (that big word means just enough and no more, please), it is very wholesome. We must learn to be expert in cooking meats and learn to eat them so slowly and carefully (chewing makes *such* a difference) that we can enjoy our portion without asking for too many helpings.

Meat is one of the most expensive foods we put on our tables. When you consider how many people must work to get it to us—the farmer, the railroad man, the stockyards people, and then the butchers, with maybe more railroad men or expressmen in between—we wonder that we can get good meat as cheaply as we do. But just the same, it is so expensive that we must make no mistakes in our cooking. Each piece of meat we cook must be cooked and served perfectly—nothing but perfection is good enough for us, is it? So, however careful we have been before, we are going to be still more particular with this chapter, because we mean to be excellent cooks and we are very much in earnest about our important business.

The cook's interest in the meat begins when it is bought. There must be enough for the number to be served—but not too much, unless, of course, it is planned to have some left over for a dish the next day. Some

of the most delicious meat dishes we have are what are called "made dishes." That means dishes made of meat that was left from another cooking. If you plan to have some left over, that is a different matter. But if not, try to order accurately. Usually it is enough to order a little more than one-quarter of a pound for each person. Now of course that varies greatly. John, who is sixteen and plays football, will quite rightly eat more meat than grandma, who does no vigorous exercising. Susan, who is three, should eat only a tiny bit, maybe not any as yet. But in the average family, one-quarter of a pound or a bit more to a person will be about the right quantity. Of course this does not mean that one person eats that much solid meat—oh, no! That includes the bone and fat and all that. What a person eats after it is all trimmed and cooked is quite a little less. We are talking about what we buy, not what we finally eat.

As soon as the meat comes from the shop, look it over carefully to make sure that it is what you bought and is satisfactory. Most butchers are very reliable, but, even so, they would rather have you look your purchase over and be sure it is right just as soon as it is delivered. This avoids a last-minute disappointment and a rush for you or the butcher boy to correct someone's mistake.

Take the meat from the wrapping paper, lay it on a plate—china or porcelain, not metal—and cover it with paraffin paper. Then put it into the ice box. Be sure you set it in the very center of the bottom of the ice box. That is the coldest place. If you notice bits of bone or loose skin or paper on the meat,

of course you will remove those before putting it away. Sometimes, in sawing the meat the bits will stick, and it is better to remove those at once so that the meat is ready for cooking when it is put away. Never wash meat for that washes away most of the flavor, too. If it seems to need it, wipe it off with a soft cloth. Meat that appears to need washing is not fit for use and should be returned at once.

It is hard to decide which to cook first, for so many kinds of meat would be good. But after much thought we have decided to cook pork chops. We can get those any time of year and in almost any place a CHILD LIFE cook happens to live. Almost everyone likes them, and you know what fun it is to have people like what you cook. And they are not too expensive. Lamb chops, which you can cook by the same method, are delicious, but at some times of the year, they are very costly. For our first meat cooking we want something not too expensive, don't we?

Buy four loin pork chops. This means that the chop is cut from the loin where the tenderloin is—a very tasty bit. Later, you can get different sorts of pork chops and cook them the same way as you now do the loin chops. Tell the butcher to cut them so that four chops weigh about one pound and three or four ounces. Then, you will have a chop big enough to serve one, and only one, to each person. If you have more people in your family, or less, get the right number. If you tell the butcher that four chops should weigh one pound and four ounces, he will know how much to give you if you want five chops or seven or two.

ITALIAN PORK CHOPS

Get out a skillet big enough to hold the number of chops you mean to cook. (If your family is *very* big, you may need two skillets! The chops must lie flat and even on the bottom.)

Put ½ cupful of sifted flour on a plate.

Measure 2 tablespoonfuls of fat—this may be lard or vegetable fat or meat drippings, whichever you can most conveniently use.

Put the fat into the skillet and melt it till it is good and hot but not smoking.

This much of your work must be done 30 minutes before dinner is to be served, so begin in time.

Take the chops from the ice box and dip them into the flour. Handle one chop at a time, being careful to flour every single bit of the surface.

Turn up the gas so that the fat is very hot.

Carefully lay the chops in the skillet. Handle one at a time and move slowly so the hot fat does not spatter.

Cover the skillet tightly and cook the chops for 4 minutes.

With a long-handled fork turn the chops, being careful to keep each in its place without piling it onto the others. If the chops do not seem brown, cook them 3 or 4 minutes longer before turning. But the heat should be great enough to brown them quickly.

Cover and cook on the second side for about the same length of time as was needed to brown the first.

Remove the cover and lift each chop to see that it does not stick.

Salt by sprinkling 1 teaspoonful of salt over the four chops—¼ teaspoonful for each chop.

Pour ½ cupful of water over the chops.

Cover tightly and cook gently for 15 minutes. The total cooking should take 25 minutes, with lower heat for the last 15 minutes. The meat should be done through, not a bit pink.

Remove to a hot platter. Serve with apple sauce (see first lesson) on the platter and a little fresh parsley for a garnish.

Serve at once.

BEEF OR LAMB WITH CARROTS

Buy 1 pound of beef from the shoulder round (or 1½ pounds of short ribs) and have it cut into small pieces about 2 inches square or a bit smaller. If you use lamb, get 1½ pounds from the breast or shoulder. You can buy less of the round of beef than of other sorts because it has less waste—that means less bone and fat—to the pound. It also costs more, so it is fair in the end.

Roll meat in flour, being sure that each piece is well covered.

Put 3 tablespoonfuls of fat into a skillet (bacon fat is fine for this) and slide in the floured pieces of meat, being careful not to spatter the hot fat.

With a fork turn them gently while they cook until every piece is nicely browned.

Add 2 cupfuls of carrots which you have previously peeled and sliced fine. (Cut them in strips or dice shape if you prefer.)

Add 1 cupful of water and 2 teaspoonfuls of salt. Cover tightly and simmer for one hour. Stir three times during the hour, just barely moving the meat enough to make sure it does not stick.

Serve hot with baked potatoes.

FRIED CHICKEN

Have the chicken dressed and cut in pieces suitable for frying. Your butcher will do this, so do not attempt to do it yourself.

Look the chicken over carefully, making sure that each piece is clean and neatly cut. Wipe dry if it seems moist

Flour it carefully just as you did the beef. That means, spread the flour on a plate and take time to see that each piece of chicken is well covered.

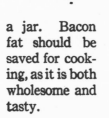

Put 4 tablespoonfuls of fat into a large skillet and melt it.

Put the chicken into the hot fat, making sure that each piece lies flat.

Brown and turn every piece until it is a rich golden brown color.

Sprinkle it with 3 teaspoonfuls of salt.

Cover the skillet tightly and draw back from the hot fire or turn down the gas, cooking slowly for 30 or 40 minutes. The length of time needed will depend on the size of the chicken. If the meat on the leg seems tender when twisted with a fork, the chicken is done.

Serve with a garnish of parsley, using mashed potatoes and a seasonable vegetable.

BEEFSTEAK BALLS

Buy 1 pound of ground beef. This should be from the round or the shoulder.

Divide into four equal parts and mold firmly into round, flat cakes about 1 inch thick.

If you prefer, you may make eight smaller cakes. These would be easier to turn in the pan. But the larger cakes look more like individual steaks.

Put a frying pan or iron skillet over the fire, and when it is smoking hot, set the cakes or meat on it. The skillet should be hot enough so that the meat begins to sizzle the instant it touches the metal.

As soon as the cakes are brown on the bottom (this will take 3 to 5 minutes) turn them with a spatula.

Sprinkle with salt, using 1 teaspoonful for the four cakes.

When brown on the second side, loosen them so they do not stick, cover tightly with a well-fitted cover, and cook slowly for 8 minutes. If your family likes meat rare, cook 2 minutes longer in browning and do not cover for longer cooking—take up as soon as well browned.

Serve at once on a hot platter.

This dish is delicious with hashed brown potatoes and broiled tomatoes.

BROILED BACON

Arrange the strips of bacon neatly on the broiler rack.

Slip them into the broiler and cook until the bacon is crisp. This will take from 5 to 10 minutes, according to the thickness of the bacon.

Take up the bacon on a hot platter. Drain the fat from the drip pan into

a jar. Bacon fat should be saved for cooking, as it is both wholesome and tasty.

PAN BROILED BACON

If you do not have a broiler or for some reason do not care to use it, bacon can be "pan-broiled" with equal success.

Heat a frying pan smoking hot.

Lower the heat and lay the bacon neatly in the hot pan.

Cook at a moderate temperature, turning once, until the bacon is crisp.

With a fork lift out the bacon, piece by piece, being careful to let the fat drip off before you put the bacon on the hot platter. This fat should also be saved for cooking.

PAN BROILED CHOPS

Prepare either lamb, pork or veal chops carefully, making sure they are dry and free from bits of bone or skin. It is important to leave the rim of fat around the edge as that is to supply the fat needed in cooking.

Heat a frying pan or iron skillet till a drop of cold water sizzles when dropped upon it.

Lay the chops on the hot surface. Use a fork and work quickly so all can begin cooking at nearly the same time.

Cook for three minutes by which time the lower side should be a dainty brown.

With a long fork, turn and brown on the second side.

Turn again and season with salt using ¼ teaspoonful for each chop.

Lower the heat considerably, cover tightly and cook longer.

Cook ten minutes additional for lamb chops, fifteen minutes for pork and twenty for veal.

Many people think pan broiling is the best of all methods for cooking chops for the quick searing keeps in all the juices and a limited amount of fat is used. On the other hand, this method does not produce the flaky dressing the flour used in the Italian style makes. A wise cook learns both methods and alternates them for variety.

LEG OF LAMB ROAST

This is the simplest of all roasts to cook and makes a fine choice for a birthday dinner for Mother if you are planning a surprise.

Buy the hind quarter and tell the butcher to trim off the coarse outside skin which he calls fell and take off the extra bone. Your roast should be from 4½ to 6½ pounds—5½ to 6 is the best. This will serve eight or nine people very generously. A smaller family will have some very nice cold meat left over and enough bits to grind and serve with rice or peas for a third meal.

As soon as you know the size of your roast, decide when you will put it on to cook. Plan to roast it for fifteen mintues in a hot oven. Then reduce the heat and roast it 15 minutes for every pound. That means that if you have a 6 pound roast, you roast it 15 minutes at a high temperature and then 6 times 15 minutes at a lower temperature—7 times 15 minutes or one hour and three quarters in all. So if dinner is at six o'clock the 6 pound roast goes into the oven at 4:15. Take a pencil and paper if you need to and figure accurately about the time so that your roast is done at exactly the right minute.

Put the roast in a roasting pan, sprinkle with 2 teaspoonfuls of salt.

Put 2 tablespoonfuls of meat drippings over the top. Bacon or sausage fat is best. If you do not have such drippings, put four slices of bacon over the top of the roast. Remove the bacon as soon as it is browned and keep it for a garnish.

At the end of the first fifteen minutes, open the oven, pull the pan to the front and pour 1 cupful of water over the roast. Lower the heat to make a very moderate oven and keep at this lower, even temperature till done.

Every 15 minutes open the oven, and with a large long handled spoon, pour some of the pan drippings back over the roast. Work quickly so as not to cool the oven.

At the end of the cooking, remove the roast to a warm platter, garnish with parsley or cress and serve with brown gravy or mint sauce.

Potatoes, carefully peeled, can be put into the roast pan one hour ahead of dinner time, and they will roast beautifully with no further trouble. Carrots, peeled and trimmed, can also be baked in the same pan and are very good with lamb. They roast in 50 minutes.

MINT SAUCE

Chop mint leaves till you have enough to make 3 tablespoonfuls.

Heat ¾ cupful vinegar to a boil.

Pour over the mint leaves and let stand fifteen minutes.

Serve warm.

VEGETABLES—POTATOES

WHAT is your favorite vegetable? That's easy to guess, for we gave it away at the top of the chapter. Potatoes, of course! Any girl or boy who doesn't like potatoes—but then there isn't any such person, so why talk about it? Everyone, big or little, old or young, likes that vegetable. Moreover, we have potatoes all the year around and we have them every day, so it is very important to know how to cook them well and in enough different ways to make a pleasing variety.

We get one of our most useful foods from potatoes—starch. Starch is the food that gives us energy. Potatoes make other valuable additions to the diet, too, such as potash and other minerals. It is interesting to know that most of these lie very close under the peeling. So when potatoes are baked, we save more of these minerals than when we peel them and cook them other ways. Therefore we want to be sure to serve baked potatoes at least twice a week. We must remember that.

Another point we want to notice is that potatoes, wholesome as they are, do not take the place of other vegetables. We must not eat just meat and potatoes at every dinner, no matter how delicious we think that menu is. We must have other kinds of vegetables so that we have a variety of minerals. If we like potatoes so well, and of course we do, we may have them every dinner provided we vary the other vegetables, using root vegetables some days and vegetables that grow in the air other days; green or yellow vegetables some days and other colored vegetables other days. Doesn't it seem funny to say that the color of a vegetable counts in planning? But, truly, it does. People who study diet all the time tell us that different colored vegetables have different food values, so when we make a meal pretty to look at by having a pleasing variety of color, we also make the meal wholesome by having a variety of nourishment. That seems very interesting, doesn't it?

Find out from Mother how she buys potatoes—cooks must learn marketing, too. If you have a nice cold cellar where things keep very well, probably Mother buys potatoes by the bushel or sack in the fall and brings them up to the pantry, a basketful at a time. Years and years ago, before there were such things as cold storage and apartment buildings, everyone bought potatoes that way. In the spring of the year, the potatoes would begin to "sprout." This means that they grow tiny vines and some warm Saturday Mother would take all the children in the family down to the cellar to rub the "sprouts" off so the potatoes couldn't grow but would stay fine for cooking and eating. Doesn't that seem funny?

But nowadays market conditions are so good that it is only people who have very good food cellars or else those who live away from markets, who buy a season's supply of potatoes in the fall. The waste of those that spoil is more than the saving of buying a lot together. People buy a small quantity at a time, a bushel or a peck or even a half-peck for a very small family. If you ask your mother or grandmother, she can tell you much more about changes in marketing from even twenty years ago. All such things are very good for a cook to know.

We are going to learn how to cook potatoes in several ways, beginning with the kind that is both the easiest and the most wholesome of all.

BAKED POTATOES

Select 6 medium-sized, well-shaped potatoes. The queer-shaped ones and the very tiny or very big ones can be used when the recipe says to peel and cut them up. For baking we want the prettiest and nicest in the whole basket.

Scrub them thoroughly with a vegetable brush.

Cut off any tiny imperfections. The potatoes should be so clean and perfect when you have finished that every speck of the peeling can be eaten after it is baked.

Have the oven moderately hot. If you use a gas oven, be sure to light the gas **before** you begin scrubbing, so that it is hot when you are ready for it.

Put the potatoes on the upper shelf; close the oven tightly and bake for 45 to 50 minutes. Look at the potatoes twice during this time to see that they are not browning too fast.

At the end of 45 minutes, push a sharp-pronged fork into one potato. If it runs in easily and the potato is soft inside, it is done. If not, cook it a few minutes more and test again.

When done, remove from the oven onto a clean towel.

With a sharp knife, cut a cross about two inches each way in the top of each potato. Give it a quick squeeze from end to end and then from side to side. Be quick so you will not burn your fingers. This squeeze loosens the inside and helps to make it mealy.

Drop a small square of butter into the very center of each potato.

Arrange them neatly on a plate or vegetable dish covered with a napkin (to absorb steam) and serve at once.

Baked potatoes should be timed so that they are done just at the right minute to serve, as they are not improved by standing. If you cannot tell just when your family will be ready for dinner (and sometimes you cannot), plan to use Stuffed Baked Potatoes rather than the plain ones, as the stuffed ones can stand quite a little while with no damage done.

Potatoes prepared and baked by this rule can be eaten to the last bit—peeling and all—and are a very wholesome and palatable food.

STUFFED BAKED POTATOES

Scrub, prepare, and bake 6 potatoes exactly as for plain Baked Potatoes. (See recipe above.)

When the potatoes are done and have been removed from the oven to a clean towel, stand each one on the flattest side so that it looks well and stands firmly. That is the bottom side.

Cut two inches off the top side—two inches long and the width of the top of the potato. You will have no further use for this piece of peeling.

With a spoon, scoop out the whole inside of the potato into a bowl. Of course the freshly baked potatoes are piping hot, so you must hold them in a small napkin lest you burn your fingers. But if they are held right and you work quickly, you can have all the potatoes emptied in short order, and have no burned fingers either.

Set the 6 empty potato shells on a pan and in a warm place. You will want them later.

Put the potato pulp through a potato ricer. If Mother has no ricer, mash them carefully with a masher or a big spoon till there are no lumps.

Add 2 tablespoonfuls of butter

    1½ teaspoonful of salt

    ⅓ cupful whole milk or cream

Beat this mixture till creamy.

Pack into the potato shells, using the whole quantity and leaving the tops a bit rough so they will brown prettily.

Put into the oven for about 10 minutes or until they are hot and browned.

MASHED POTATOES

Wash, peel, and cut into pieces the equivalent of 6 medium-sized potatoes. The pieces should be about the size of an egg. Drop peeled potatoes into cold water while you are working so that they will not get brown.

Put into a saucepan and cover with 1 quart of boiling water.

Cook about 23 minutes, boiling rapidly. Test with a fork and if they are tender, remove them at once from the flame. Potatoes should be tender but not cooked mushy.

Pour into a colander that is set over a pan or bowl. Save the water in which the potatoes were

L.K.D.

cooked for soup as it has valuable food properties.

Put the drained potatoes through a ricer, dropping them into a mixing bowl or mash thoroughly with a masher.

Add two tablespoonfuls butter
   1½ teaspoonfuls salt
   ⅓ cupful milk or cream

Beat all till creamy. If mixture is too stiff to beat well, add ¼ cupful more milk. You may have taken a little more potato than this recipe intended, but that will be all right if you add a little more milk and seasoning.

Set over the oven or a low flame till the potatoes are steaming hot.

Serve at once. Garnish with parsley cut fine.

If for any reason the meal is delayed, mashed potatoes can be kept hot over a pan of hot water—like a double boiler.

Leftover mashed potatoes can be made at once into small, flat cakes and at a later meal—breakfast or luncheon—you can brown them in butter or meat drippings and serve them piping hot. These easily prepared Mashed Potato Cakes are delicious.

PLAIN BOILED POTATOES

Wash and peel 6 even-sized potatoes. If they are very small, use 12 or more.

Put into a saucepan, cover with a quart of boiling water, and boil briskly for 30 minutes. A longer time is needed because the potatoes are not cut up as in the mashed potato recipe. If you have used small potatoes, cooking will take less time.

Drain off the water and save it for soup.

Return potatoes to the pan and sprinkle with 2 teaspoonfuls of salt.

Drop 2 tablespoonfuls of butter (cut into small pieces) over them.

Shake briskly over the fire for 2 minutes till salt and butter covers all.

Take up in a warm dish and garnish with parsley.

HASHED BROWN POTATOES

Leftover boiled potatoes may be used for this recipe or potatoes may be freshly boiled just for this use.

Chop or dice fine with a knife enough cold, cooked potatoes to make 3 cupfuls. (Of course you need more for a big family.

Melt 3 tablespoonfuls of butter or meat drippings in a frying pan. Vegetable oil may also be used.

Slide the potatoes into the hot fat and brown with moderately slow cooking. This will take at least 10 minutes.

With a pancake turner or a spatula turn the potatoes, being careful not to make them mushy.

Brown the potatoes again, loosen from the pan when browned.

Pour ½ cupful milk over them; cover tightly and cook with a slow fire for 5 minutes.

GERMAN FRIED POTATOES

Wash, peel, and slice enough potatoes to make 3 cupfuls—piled-up measurement.

Melt 3 tablespoonfuls of butter or other fat into an iron skillet.

Slide in the raw, sliced potatoes.

Cover tightly and cook 25 minutes, turning with a pancake turner three times during the cooking so that all will become well browned. This is a very good dish to be served with ham or chops.

FRENCH FRIED POTATOES

Peel four large potatoes or the equivalent in smaller potatoes.

Cut them into strips two and one half to three inches long and slightly larger than your little finger.

Wash twice in cold water and drain.

Wrap in a dry towel for fifteen minutes or longer. This absorbs the moist starch on the potato and makes them fry much better than if they were wet and freshly peeled.

Measure 2 cupfuls of fat or vegetable oil and put into a small, deep frying pan. The deeper your pan the less fat will be needed for fine results in frying. Remember, this fat will not be used up—you should have almost as much left after frying as at first.

Heat the fat till it is smoking hot.

Put the potatoes into a wire basket and lower into the fat. Some cooks do not use a basket, but drop the potatoes directly into the fat. This is all right except there is danger of burning the hand from splashing. The basket is both safer and neater.

Cook till the potatoes are a beautiful golden brown. This should take about 20 minutes.

Lift up the basket and drain off the fat.

Salt the potatoes by shaking over them ¾ teaspoon salt.

Serve at once. These potatoes are particularly fine with creamed meat dishes or with chops.

OTHER VEGETABLES

VEGETABLES are one of our most important foods. They have wonderful minerals which make us strong and healthy. They help to give us good teeth and pink cheeks. Therefore every cook must know how to prepare and serve them at their best.

You should select vegetables with great care, making sure that they are fresh and in excellent condition. Sometimes wilted vegetables can be revived by fresh water and ice, but generally poor or wilted vegetables are a waste and consequently an extravagance instead of an economy.

As soon as vegetables are delivered, look them over and put them away. Root vegetables should be put into tidy boxes in a cool place. Never let things stand around in bags—they look so mussy. Leaf vegetables and all vegetables that grow above the ground should be washed and put in a cool place. It is better to wrap them in moist cloths and put them into the ice box. This means lettuce, celery, asparagus, spinach, and all such vegetables. Corn should be put away in a cool, dark place and husked just before cooking, as it hardens quickly when exposed to the air.

Always use boiling water—that means, have the water boiling when it is put on the vegetables—and use as little as possible. The minerals we spoke of above dissolve into the water, and if that is poured off into the sink, much of the value of eating vegetables is lost. Isn't that foolish? Careful cooks use slow cooking, very little water—just enough so that it boils down, and what tiny bit is left can be served with the vegetable. Always add the salt five minutes before the cooking is finished.

Serve all vegetables very hot and with only butter and salt for seasoning. It used to be the custom to make rich and thick cream sauces for vegetables. But though occasionally some sauces are still used, most people prefer the vegetable plain. If it has been properly cooked it is most delicious that way.

If you live where you can have a garden, it is fun to raise some of your own vegetables. Nothing tastes better than a vegetable you have grown and gathered yourself.

If you live in the city where you cannot possibly have a garden of your own, get your family to drive you out to the truck garden district that lies outside each big city so you can see the vegetables growing. They taste so much better when you know how pretty they look in the gardens.

For our first lesson we are going to cook asparagus. If you begin cooking at a time of year when asparagus is not in the market, use canned asparagus, beginning your work where the recipe says, "Cook 5 minutes more." Put the asparagus and its juice in a saucepan and cook 5 minutes. From there, follow the recipe.

Select the asparagus with great care, making sure that it is clean, crisp, and not too green. As soon as it is delivered, wash it, being careful to remove all sand from the tiny cracks, and put it into a cheesecloth bag beside the ice. We save our sugar bags for vegetables. They are just the right size.

When it is almost time to cook the asparagus, take it from the ice box, remove it from the bag, and break off the coarse, woody ends. These are not good to eat. To do this, pick up the first piece of asparagus and bend it about an inch from the big end. Does it seem crisp and snappy? Then that end is fine to eat, and it is not necessary to take any off. Does it seem tough? Then bend it a little higher up. Bend firmly, and it will snap right off at the end of the hard, woody part. After you have done a few stalks you can easily tell what part to take off and what is good to leave for eating. Now for our recipe.

BUTTERED ASPARAGUS

Wash and chill two bunches of asparagus
Remove woody ends and wash again
Put 1 cupful of water on to boil in a tall narrow pan. (One like the top part of a double boiler is best, for then the bottom end of the stalks are really in the water while the tender tops cook just by steam.)

When the water comes to a boil, drop in the asparagus, a few stalks at a time. Be careful to put the ends of the stalks down. The tender tips should never be in the water.

Cover very tightly and cook for 25 minutes.

Remove cover and test with a fork. The best way is to remove one stalk, cool it a few seconds, and then see if the tough end is tender. If it is not, cook 5 minutes more. By this time the water will be almost gone.

Sprinkle 1 teaspoon salt over the asparagus. Cover tightly and remove from the fire while you arrange triangles of toast (which you have made while the asparagus was cooking) on a warm platter or on individual plates.

With a fork, take up the asparagus and arrange it neatly, stalks all lying the same way, on the toast. Divide it fairly so that all can be equally served.

Put 1 teaspoonful of butter for each person served into the water gravy left in the pan, melt quickly, and pour in equal portions over the asparagus.

Serve at once.

If it should happen that the water so nearly boils away that you have no gravy, drop the piece of butter directly on the asparagus and the steam will melt it in.

Be sure to notice the small quantity of water used. This method keeps all the fine minerals that are so wholesome and tasty. But you must be careful not to use too high a flame for cooking lest your water vanish too soon. You want it to last just the half hour of cooking—no less.

When asparagus season is over, you can use this same method for cooking dainty little green onions. You know the kind we eat raw usually? They are delicious cooked this way and served with butter on toast. Young carrots are fine, too. Scrape them and cook them in just a little bit of water and serve with salt and butter exactly as you do the asparagus, only you may prefer to omit the toast.

If you happen to be where you cannot get fresh vegetables, use canned ones, heating them until they boil for 5 minutes, then serving them exactly as you would the fresh vegetables.

Speaking of vegetables reminds us that a vegetable luncheon is very good. How does this menu sound to you?

SPRING LUNCHEON
Tomato bouillon
Cheese wafers

Buttered asparagus   Baked potatoes
Radishes   Tiny onions

- - - -

Strawberry shortcake
Milk

BUTTERED BEETS

Wash 2 bunches of young beets. Trim off leaves 2 inches from the root.

Cover with 1 quart of boiling water. Beets are cooked with skins on, so you can take plenty of water and throw it out when finished. The minerals are not lost as in peeled vegetables.

Cover beets tightly and boil them until tender when pricked with a fork. It will take 45 or 55 minutes, according to the size of the beets.

Pour off water and set beets under cold running water until they are cool enough to handle.

Rub off the skins. This is easily done without a knife.

With a knife trim off all blemishes.

Put the beets with 2 tablespoonfuls of butter, 2 of water, and 1 teaspoonful salt into a saucepan.

Cover tightly until they are again heated through.

Serve in a warm dish and pour the butter sauce over the top.

Leftover beets may be sliced and covered with vinegar as a relish for the next day's dinner.

CARROTS

Scrape a dozen young carrots and cut them in strips or slices.

Add 1 cupful of boiling water.

Cook at a moderate temperature for about 30 minutes. Be sure they are *tightly* covered so that the water does not boil away. Better look a couple of times to make sure that they are not sticking to the bottom of the pan.

Five minutes before they have finished add 1 teaspoonful salt

2 tablespoonfuls butter

Serve very hot.

Leftover carrots are good in a vegetable salad or to add to a meat dish or soup.

CORN ON THE COB

While a large kettleful of water is coming to a boil, husk the corn and carefully remove all silks.

Thirteen minutes before dinner time, drop the corn into the pot, being careful not to spatter the hot water.

Cook 12 minutes after the water begins to boil again. If the water was briskly boiling when you put the corn in, it will quickly boil again.

With a long fork remove the corn from the kettle and serve at once with butter and salt.

BROILED TOMATOES

Wash 4 fine large tomatoes and cut in halves, crosswise.

Arrange them on a flat pan with the cut sides up. Sprinkle them with a bit of salt.

Set them under a broiling flame—about 2 inches from the flame. Have the oven hot.

Cook for 12 minutes.

With a pancake turner, remove tomatoes from the pan and serve at once.

These are very nice for luncheon or with beefsteak for dinner.

If you have no broiler, butter an iron skillet and cook the tomatoes on that. This will take the same time, but the tomatoes must be turned once during the cooking. Do not cover them.

ESCALLOPED CABBAGE

Cut a head of cabbage in half, through the core. Wrap one half in a damp cloth and put in a cool place for later use. Cut the remaining half into two parts.

Hold the quarter of a cabbage head firmly and slice downward with a sharp knife so that the whole amount is cut into dainty shreds. Repeat with the second quarter.

Plunge the shredded cabbage into cold water for ten or fifteen minutes while you make further preparations for the cooking.

Butter a baking dish and measure out 2 cupfuls of milk, ⅓ cupful flour, 1 teaspoonful salt, 2 tablespoonfuls butter.

Drain the cabbage in a colander or sieve.

Arrange a layer of cabbage in the dish and season with ⅓ the flour, butter and salt.

Repeat with a second and third layer.

Pour the milk over the top and bake for 40 minutes in a moderate oven.

Grated cheese over the top is a nice addition to this dish.

CAULIFLOWER

Wash and trim off the greenest and coarsest of the outside leaves of a fine head of cauliflower.

Put upside down in cold water and let stand for one hour. If you suspect that there are insects on the cauliflower, put 2 tablespoonfuls of vinegar in the water in which it is soaking.

Bring to a boil 3 pints of water and, when boiling, put in the cauliflower. Use a narrow kettle or pan so that the cauliflower will keep right side up. This means the white, flower-side, up. The stems and bottom part will need hotter cooking and should therefore be at the bottom.

Cook for 25 to 35 minutes. The time varies according to the size of the vegetable. When done, it will be tender when pricked with a fork. Do not cook too long. Over-long cooking turns the vegetable an ugly brown and spoils the delicate flavor.

Drop 2 large slices of stale bread or crusts into the water in which the cauliflower is boiled. This will absorb the odors of cooking. Keep the kettle tightly covered the whole time.

At the end of 20 minutes' cooking, add 2 teaspoonfuls of salt to the water.

When done, remove to a warm serving dish. Dot the top with 1 tablespoonful of butter, cut into bits, and serve at once.

Left-over cauliflower may be cut into small pieces and cooked exactly as escalloped cabbage only, as it has already been cooked, it needs only 20 minutes for browning. Grated cheese is a fine addition to this dish.

STRING OR WAX BEANS

Break the beans into three or four sections, carefully removing any string.

Wash in two changes of water. If the beans are sandy, as they always are when picked after a shower, wash in additional changes of water till every bit of grit is removed.

Put into a small kettle or sauce pan and cover with boiling water. Be sure the water comes up over the beans.

Add 1 teaspoonful of salt to each quart of beans.

Bring to a quick boil then cook more slowly for 25 minutes. If the beans are a bit old, cook ten minutes longer and they will be as good as young ones.

Drain, pour into a hot serving dish, dot with butter and serve at once.

PEAS

Hull as many peas as you intend to cook. Usually one allows 1 cupful (after hulling) for every three persons but the amount varies according to the size of the portion you allow each person.

Wash the hulled peas in two changes of cold water.

Put them into a small kettle and cover with boiling water. Use once and a half as much water as peas. That means, for a cupful of hulled peas, use 1½ cupfuls of boiling water. For this amount use ½ teaspoonful of salt.

Bring to a brisk boil. Then boil slowly till the peas are tender which will take about 20 minutes.

Drain through a wire sieve. Turn into a hot serving dish. Put 2 teaspoonfuls of butter on top of the peas and serve immediately.

This vegetable is delicious with chops or with egg dishes.

SPINACH

Wash the spinach in two changes of water.

Cut off the root ends and cut each group of leaves into three or more sections.

Wash again in three changes of water so as to make sure no sand remains.

Put into a sauce pan and set over a very slow fire. Use no water. Cover closely.

Cook thus very slowly for 8 minutes. By that time the juice will have drawn out and there will be plenty of water in the pan for cooking.

Boil for 15 minutes. Salt with 1 teaspoonful salt for each ½ peck of spinach (measured before preparing of course).

Drain and serve in a hot dish.

Garnish with slices of cold boiled egg or with bits of sliced carrots.

Be sure to save any juice left in the kettle. That is as valuable as anything in your kitchen for it is full of minerals, especially iron. Add it to soup. If you were careful in washing the spinach, there will not be much water left—only enough for proper cooking.

FRIED EGG PLANT

Egg plant cooked by this recipe is very nice for the main dish in a vegetable dinner because it is very attractive looking and can be served on a platter and garnished like a meat dish.

Peel an egg plant and cut it crosswise into slices about ¾ inch thick.

Put into running water for ten minutes while you make other preparations. If you haven't running water handy, use two changes of cold water, five minutes each.

Beat together 1 egg, 1 teaspoonful salt, 1 tablespoonful milk and pour into a flat dish.

Roll crackers fine enough to make 1 cupful of crumbs and put onto a large plate.

Put 4 tablespoonfuls of meat drippings or other fat into a large frying pan and heat slowly.

Cut the egg plant slices into smaller pieces for ease in handling—each slice will make two or three portions.

Now you are ready for actual cooking.

Dip a piece of egg plant into the egg mixture and cover well, each side. Lift out (use a fork) and drain while you count five. Dip quickly into the crumbs and cover on both sides. Put into the frying pan.

Repeat till the pan is full. Keep at a moderate temperature till all are ready for cooking.

Brown on one side. Turn with a spatula and brown the second side.

Cover tightly and cook at low temperature for 15 minutes.

Serve at once on a hot platter. Chili sauce is a very good relish with this dish.

HOT BREADS

NOW we are going to bake something—really, truly bake, with an oven and pans and mixing bowls and all the frills of real baking. Don't you think that will be fun? Baking is such an important form of chemistry—it always seems like magic to me! You put pans of gooey looking dough, that no one could possibly eat, into the oven; and then quietly, behind that closed door, heat changes and changes the dough till it turns into food—luscious smelling, delicious tasting food that will give pleasure in the eating and will make strong, healthy girls and boys. Can you think of anything more important to learn than just that sort of chemistry?

If you intend to be first-class cooks —as, of course, you all do—you will want to learn much more about baking than you have time for in this one lesson. You will want to learn what sort of pans are best to use, how to manage an oven, how to tell when the temperature is the right heat for what you want to bake, what kinds of foods bake best and why, and many other such facts. You won't learn them all in a day or even a year. We're all still learning. But, by being on the lookout, you can learn from magazines, from many books, and from talking with people who have been baking for more years than you have yet had a chance to work. And if you want to ask questions about things ask experienced cooks, you know—Mother and Auntie or a friend.

And now for the baking!

We are going to bake muffins. Our recipe will make twelve medium-sized muffins, so you will want two sets of muffin rings with six rings to a set. Maybe the ones your mother has are eight small rings in a set (some people call them *pans* or *tins*, but *rings* sound prettier, don't you think?); that is all right, for a recipe that will make twelve will make sixteen smaller ones quite as well.

See that the rings are clean and dry. Then grease them ready to use. Put one tablespoonful of fat into a small cup or bowl. Use vegetable oil or any good cooking fat—not butter, for it has salt in it and will make the muffins stick. Crumble a piece of fresh, white tissue paper and dip it into the fat; then run it over every bit of the inside of every ring. Be sure every bit of surface is covered well. It is a good idea to do this before you start to actually mix your dough; then the rings are ready when you want to use them.

A good cook (and of course that means you) always plans to do odd jobs like pan greasing ahead of time. Then when the mixing begins, there is no small job to delay the work.

Muffins take about 25 minutes to bake and ought to be eaten while fresh and hot. Put them into the oven exactly one-half hour before mealtime. That will give you 5 minutes for taking them from the rings to the basket or plate. Perhaps you will need as long as 30 minutes for mixing your dough, so start one hour before mealtime.

MUFFINS

Put into a mixing bowl ½ cupful sugar
    1 egg (both the yellow and white)
    ½ teaspoonful salt
    ½ cupful fat (butter, vegetable oil, or fat)
Beat this until creamy.

Add 1 cupful of whole milk. (If you used butter, skimmed milk will do.)

Add 2 cupfuls of flour into which you have sifted 4 level teaspoonfuls of baking powder.

Beat these together until smooth.

Drop this batter from a spoon into greased muffin rings.

Bake for about 25 minutes in a moderate oven. Serve immediately.

"But how shall we tell whether they are done?"

We're just coming to that. When your muffins have been in the oven 8 minutes, open the door very gently and peek. If they are baking right, they will be puffy and big, but not one bit brown. Wait another 8 minutes and peek again. By now they should begin to brown and the little mountain at the top will be splitting open and white dough will be coming through. Shut the door gently and wait 8 minutes more. Now they will look brown and ready to eat. Tap the top of the muffin nearest you—tap quickly and you will not burn your finger. If you can see the print of where your finger tapped, let the muffins bake four minutes more and test again. If you *cannot* see where you tapped, take them from the oven at once. Turn upside down on a rack on a clean towel. The muffins will drop out of the rings as quickly as you please.

BRAN MUFFINS

If your family likes bran muffins (and they are delicious, don't you think?), use 1 cupful of white flour and 1 cupful of bran in this same recipe. Sift the baking powder with the white flour, and then with a fork, thoroughly mix the cupful of bran in with the flour and baking powder. Bran, being so coarse, is not to be sifted. Or for cornmeal muffins take a cupful of cornmeal instead of the bran. And for variety, you may like to add a few chopped dates or raisins.

CORN GEMS

Put into a mixing bowl 1 tablespoonful sugar
    ½ teaspoonful salt
    1 egg (both white and yellow parts)
    3 tablespoonfuls vegetable fat
Stir until well blended.
Sift 1 teaspoonful baking powder and
    ½ teaspoonful soda into
    1 cupful flour

Put this mixture and 1 cupful cornmeal on top of the egg mixture.

Around the side of the flour pour 1 cupful sour milk.

Beat the whole until it is smooth and creamy. By adding the flour and milk in this way you can stir gradually, putting into the mixture a little more of the flour every time your spoon goes around.

Drop into buttered muffin rings which you have prepared before you started just as for Muffins.

Bake 20 minutes in a hot oven.

If you have no sour milk or buttermilk, use sweet milk and omit the soda and add 1 more teaspoonful baking powder.

RICE MUFFINS

Into a mixing bowl put ⅓ cupful sugar
    1 egg (both white and yellow)
    ½ teaspoonful salt
    ⅓ cupful fat (vegetable oil or butter)
Beat until creamy.
Add 1 cupful milk.

Onto a plate sift 1 cupful of flour with 3 teaspoonfuls of baking powder.

Onto this flour put 1 cupful cooked rice.

Toss the rice gently with the flour, using a fork, till every grain of rice is covered with flour.

Add rice and flour to the dough and stir until well blended.

Drop into buttered muffin rings and bake 25 minutes. If you use very small rings bake only 20 minutes.

These muffins make a nice change and it is a fine way to use up a cupful of leftover rice.

BAKING POWDER BISCUITS

Sift together twice, 2 cupfuls flour
    ½ teaspoonful salt
    4 teaspoonfuls baking powder
With the tips of your fingers work in 6 level tablespoonfuls of lard or 5 of butter. Other fat,

such as a vegetable fat, may be used if preferred. Rub the tips of your fingers together, rubbing the fat into the flour till it all looks like a fine meal. The first few times you do this it may seem to be a slow job. So start in time and be sure to work in a cool place, for biscuit dough should be kept cool. If you begin ahead of time, you can now set the mixture aside in a cool place until about half an hour before mealtime.

Sprinkle ½ cupful of flour on a bread board.

Measure ¾ cupful of milk. Pour ½ cupful of this onto dough, tossing it with a fork so that it mixes. NEVER STIR BISCUIT DOUGH. It is impossible to tell exactly how much milk to use because of the difference in flour. So add ½ cupful first and then, if the dough seems stiff, add the rest.

The dough should be soft but not runny.

Drop the ball of dough onto the floured bread board.

With floured fingers, pat gently until it is only about ¾-inch high. Do not roll, just pat firmly but gently.

With a floured biscuit cutter, cut into small biscuits. Be careful to cut right at the tip edge of the dough each time and to fit the point left over back into the main dough. In this way you will have very few scraps of dough left. Scraps can be re-shaped and used but are not quite so nice, as they have to be worked and handled more. Biscuit dough must be handled as little as possible.

Set neatly on floured pans and bake for 12 minutes in a very hot oven.

Arrange on a napkin in a bread basket, cover with another napkin, and serve immediately.

The biscuits will be so good that four-year-old sister will be sure to want some. Tell Mother that if she will use vegetable fat in this biscuit dough and take ⅛ less than usual, and add ½ teaspoonful of baking powder to each cupful of flour she takes, she will have a flaky pastry that will make dumplings so wholesome even four-year-old sister can eat them.

Good luck with the biscuits! Remember that "good luck" means measuring accurately, following rules, and paying attention as you work.

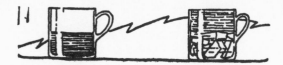

GINGERBREAD

Put together in a mixing bowl ½ cupful butter (see illustration for correct way to measure butter accurately.)

   ½ cupful sugar
   2 eggs (both yellow and white)
   1 teaspoonful ground cinnamon
   2 teaspoonfuls ground ginger

Beat until smooth and creamy. Be careful to beat slowly at first so the spices do not brush out of your bowl.

Add 1 cupful of cooking molasses and beat again.

Grease a large, flat baking pan with meat fat or vegetable oil.

See that your oven is heated ready for baking.

Sift 3 cupfuls of white flour, twice.

Measure a cupful of boiling water and dissolve 2 teaspoonfuls of baking soda in this. Hold it over your mixing bowl while doing this so that any splash is caught in the dough instead of lost.

Stir in the water and then add the sifted flour.

Beat until smooth and well blended. Then pour into the greased baking pan being sure that the dough is spread evenly into the corners.

Bake about 35 minutes in a moderate oven. Test as directed in other recipes to be sure it is done.

After taking from the oven, let the gingerbread stand for 3 minutes, then cut in large squares (while still in the pan) and serve at once. Some cooks prefer to break the bread rather than cut it while hot.

This bread is good either hot or cold. Apple sauce or baked apples served with gingerbread make a fine combination.

OTHER HOT BREADS

If you carefully follow the methods used in these few recipes, you can make any hot bread recipe you find and want to try, for the principles are the same in all—only the kind and proportion of ingredients vary.

By now, you know so much about cooking that you can cook more than half of this dinner menu:

DINNER
Cream of spinach soup
Little sausages with mashed potato
Cauliflower au gratin
Bran muffins   Jelly
Orange salad
Apple dumplings

SALADS

THE first thing in this cooking lesson is a riddle. I hope you are good at guessing, for here it is: When is cooking *not* cooking?

You guessed that right away. Yes, the answer is, "When it is salad making." Now though salad making is a very important part of cooking, it isn't really truly cooking at all, for salad is eaten raw. But it has to be prepared very carefully and served exactly right. So it is a kind of cooking, even though it isn't done on a stove.

We are making orange salad to-day and we are going to make it so perfectly that we can serve it for the family dinner or for Sunday evening tea. Maybe we shall make it several times—practice makes perfect, you know.

"How did you ever think up anything as good as orange salad?" asks somebody.

That's easy to answer. It's our business to know what people like to eat and when they want it. And almost everyone knows that oranges taste very, very fine any time of year. You know how it is, some days are so hot you don't feel hungry —eat an orange and you want more. Or maybe it's dark and rainy—one of those cold spring rains that make the tulips bow clear down to the ground. That's the very time for the cook to get out her oranges, for their color is so sunny and cheerful and their taste so refreshing. Then there are winter days so stormy and cold that you think you just must have oranges, and plenty of them, to make you feel your best.

So you see, it's very important that Child Life Cooks shall learn to make something from oranges.

Moreover, they must learn to peel oranges so skillfully that they can always do it without the least muss or bother.

Perhaps it would be a good idea to practice peeling oranges before we actually start making salad. We are planning for six people to-day, so we shall need three oranges. We shall peel those first and make the salad afterward.

First, wash your hands very carefully, with especial attention to the cleaning of nails. The cook who works with oranges should be very dainty and neat.

With a tin spoon, cut a circle the size of a nickel in the stem end of an orange. If there is no tin spoon handy, use a thin silver spoon or a dull silver knife. But a tin spoon is best. Take away this circle of peel and pick off the white pith underneath.

Now, with your thumbs, loosen the peeling down the sides of the orange— loosen it in about five strips and gradually push the peeling away until you get down and down and down the sides, and the orange lies like a ball in a loose jacket of peeling.

Lift the orange entirely out of the peeling and then pick off every bit of the white pith. That wasn't hard, was it?

With practice you can learn to do it without losing one drop of juice or even dampening your fingers. Try again with the second orange and then the third and by that time you will do it very well, indeed.

Put the oranges on a plate in a cool place; wash your hands and put the peelings in the garbage and you are ready for the main part of the lesson.

ORANGE SALAD

Peel and chill 3 oranges.

Wash and pick over one head of lettuce. Put the leaves in a moist cloth bag or roll in a clean wet dish towel for an hour. This will make them firm and crisp.

Measure into a small bowl:

1 teaspoonful sugar
½ teaspoonful salt
¼ teaspoonful paprika
½ cupful salad oil
¼ cupful white vinegar or lemon juice

Put in ice box to chill.

Fifteen minutes before mealtime get out six salad plates and arrange the lettuce leaves on them in the shape of little nests.

If Mother allows you to use a knife, cut the oranges in thin slices and put the equivalent of half an orange on each nest. If Mother would rather you did not use a sharp knife, separate each orange into sections, without breaking, and arrange half of each orange on each lettuce nest just the same as if the sections were slices.

Stir the dressing until the oil is well mixed and with a spoon, drip it over each plate of salad. Divide the ¾ cupful as equally as you can among your six plates.

Serve at once with salt crackers or cheese wafers.

RUSSIAN SALAD

This is a very good dinner salad.

Arrange nest of washed and chilled lettuce as before.

Make a dressing as follows:

Chop fine 1 hard boiled, chilled egg, and put it into a mixing bowl.

Over this pour ⅓ cupful of mayonnaise (salad dressing can be purchased ready made and at moderate cost, it is probably better for you to use that instead of attempting to make your own mayonnaise just yet.)

¼ cupful chili sauce

½ teaspoonful salt
2 tablespoonfuls chopped sweet pepper.

Mix together gently until thoroughly blended.

Drip over the hearts of lettuce just before serving.

BANANA SALAD

Wash, pick over, and chill 1 choice head of lettuce according to directions given for orange salad.

Just at mealtime, arrange lettuce in pretty nests on individual plates or fix the nests, one for each person, on a larger salad service.

Cut 4 peeled and chilled bananas (one for each person) into halves lengthwise and crosswise.

Arrange the quarters with the round sides up on the lettuce nests.

Make a French dressing as for Orange Salad and at the last minute drip it over the salad.

A sweet or plain wafer is better than a salt wafer for this salad. A fruit salad is very good for the last course of a meal, as it has some of the advantages of both dessert and salad.

With these directions for the lettuce—which is the foundation for every salad—and with these three kinds of dressings (French dressing as for Orange Salad, Russian dressing, and ready-made mayonnaise) you can make many kinds of salad.

For instance:

PINEAPPLE AND CHEESE SALAD

On nests of chilled lettuce arrange slices of chilled pineapple, using one slice for each person.

Roll cream cheese into little balls about the size of a large marble and then roll them in finely chopped nuts. Set in the center of the pineapple, covering the hole.

Use French dressing.

CHEESE AND DATE SALAD

Remove the seeds from enough dates to allow 3 for each person.

Make two cheese balls per person (from soft cream cheese as in the Pineapple Salad) and leave them plain or roll them in chopped nuts as you prefer.

Arrange the dates and cheese balls on nests of lettuce and serve with either French or Mayonnaise dressing. If there is a dessert course to follow, the French dressing is better, as it is not so rich. But if the salad is not followed by dessert it is nice to use mayonnaise.

DESSERTS—FRUIT DISHES

NOW we have cooked the first three courses of our dinner and are ready for dessert. Maybe you used to think dessert was the best part of the meal. But now that you have learned to cook the three other courses yourself, surely you think they are every bit as good—maybe better. But you like dessert just the same, don't you? So we must learn many kinds of dessert and cook them well so that you can know a great variety of goodies with which to finish off a dinner.

Suppose we first talk for a few minutes about what dessert is. It is the end of the meal, a tasty bite for the last, as it were. It must be very, very good, for no one is really hungry by now and only something that is very good will be enjoyed.

It must not be too rich. You have eaten the main part of your food, and if you follow with too rich a dessert you will feel heavy and tired (on account of the extra work of digesting too much) instead of happy and satisfied as you ought to be at the end of dinner. The portions must not be too large. Maybe you still feel that you could "eat a lot," but most people prefer modest portions of dessert. Try to learn just the right quantity that your family will enjoy; you do not want to seem stingy nor do you want good food left over to be thrown out.

If your dinner has rather less than the usual portion of starches, you can use a sweet dessert. This means that if you do not have potatoes, or if you have no hot bread and only a little cold bread, or if you have a thin soup instead of a rich soup,

you may serve a sweet pudding, a pastry, or some such dessert at the end of the meal. If you had muffins or biscuits, or maybe a good dish of potatoes and also rolls, you must not have any starch in the dessert because there was plenty in the earlier courses. A good cook is very careful to plan her menus this way when she wishes to serve her family the right quantity of the different sorts of foods each day—just the right quantity and no more.

If the first part of your dinner has had plenty of starch, use a fruit dessert—one that is made of just fruits in some form or one that is made with gelatine. A fruit dessert can be very attractive and delicious, yet it is both easy to make and wholesome, for it is not heavy. Because desserts are of so many sorts, we are taking three chapters for that course, so when you have finished them, you will know many kinds.

For our first dessert we are going to make something that can be used not only as a dessert for dinner but for a luncheon dessert, or as a first course at a company Sunday breakfast as well. And because the dish is so *very* good, we will call it AMBROSIA. You know in fairy tales that is the name of the food kings and queens and princes always eat.

To make ambrosia, you must use four kinds of fruit, and three of the four kinds must be juicy so you will have plenty of liquid. You must have at least one more fruit for a garnish—two would be still prettier. How many kinds of fruit can you name? Apples, oranges, grapefruit, bananas, dates cherries, cocoanut, pears, peaches, and apricots, we can think of easily. Plums and all sorts of berries are fruits, but they are not quite as nice for ambrosia as the others, so I would not use them unless I could not get four fruits from the first list. Always use at least one, and better, two raw fruits. Nuts are a kind of fruit too—they grow on trees; and they make a fine garnish even though we do not usually think of them as fruit.

AMBROSIA

Select four kinds of fruit. Cut into small pieces enough to make ½ cupful of each kind. Measure the fruit without the juice and then add juice enough to fill all the cracks.

Add ¼ cupful of sugar to each raw fruit. (The cooked fruits will need no sugar.)

Pour all four of the half cupfuls into a bowl and set in a cool place to chill.

When ready to serve put this mixture into individual glasses. This recipe will serve four.

Garnish with grated cocoanut and a candied cherry, or with chopped dates and nuts.

Serve with tiny cakes or sweet wafers.

To prepare the grapefruit or orange, peel carefully, being sure to remove all the white pith, just as in making orange salad. Loosen each section of fruit by running a sharp knife lengthwise along the section of white skin. After it is loosened, the whole section of fine fruit will pull out right from the core and will be free from both seeds and skin.

To fix the apple, pare, cut into four sections, and cut off the core. Dice the fruit into a cup and squeeze the juice of half a lemon over the fruit. This will improve the flavor and will also keep it from turning yellow-brown while you are fixing the other fruits. Bananas are peeled, cut fine, and sprinkled with a bit of lemon juice, too.

To prepare canned fruit, drain the pieces of fruit from the juice. Cut fine into a cup and then cover with juice. If any juice is left over, it can be used for gelatine or in salad dressing.

If you are having company for over Sunday, we think this would be a good menu for Sunday morning breakfast:

Ambrosia
Oatmeal with cream
Tomato omelet
Muffins
Milk

Or you can use Ambrosia for dessert at Sunday dinner and have plain sliced oranges for the fruit course at breakfast. Isn't it convenient to know how to make a dish that fits in different meals so well?

After you have made Ambrosia several times, as of course you will, try making up a fruit combination of your own. An original recipe is great fun to do, and by now you are getting so experienced that you should make very good ones.

BERRIES

Berries of all sorts are very nice for dessert. But they must be fresh and perfect and well served, so you must be just as particular with them as if you were preparing an elaborate cooked dessert.

As soon as berries are delivered from the market, they should be emptied from their boxes onto large plates. Do not allow the berries to pile up, for then they will get mashed. Take at least one large dinner plate for each boxful. Remove any spoiled or crushed berries. Put the plates of berries in the ice box at once.

Just before mealtime, prepare the berries for serving.

STRAWBERRIES

With a small, sharp knife cut off the hull, removing at the same time any hard end that may be just under the hull. If the berry is perfectly ripe, there will be no hard place.

Then remove any imperfection.

Drop the berries into a colander or large sieve.

When all are looked over and hulled, dip the sieve or colander into a deep pan of cold water. Lift the colander up and down a couple of times. Then change the water and repeat. This washes the berries without crushing them either with running water or your fingers.

Drain at once and put the berries into individual dishes or a large serving dish. Keep very cool.

OTHER BERRIES

Blackberries, raspberries—red, white, and black—and huckleberries are marketed without their stems. So these merely have to be picked over to remove imperfect fruit. It is wise to watch carefully for insects, especially when fixing raspberries.

Wash and serve as you did strawberries.

Sugar to taste should be added at the table, never ahead of serving, as it draws out the juice and makes the berries look mushy.

DESSERTS—GELATINE

OUR second lesson on desserts is to be about the kinds that are made with gelatine. You will like doing these for many reasons. First, they are good to eat, second, they are very wholesome, and you can eat plenty of them after a big dinner and still not eat too much; third, you can make them ahead of time. This last is a great advantage, especially if you are getting all or most all of the dinner. Hot things simply must be cooked at the last minute, and it is an excellent idea to have the dessert all ready. Then, all you have to remember is to get it from the ice box and take it to the table when you are through with the other courses.

Of course just gelatine and gelatine and gelatine, wouldn't please your family very well. Families always insist on variety. You must learn a great many kinds of gelatine desserts. Some of them are so different from others that you yourself would hardly guess they were made in a similar way.

Another point you must study is the form of serving gelatine. Sometimes you will use Mother's big ring mold. Next time, take a deep, round bowl. Another day use individual molds, and another time mold the mixture in a broad, flat pan or dish and with a fancy shaped cutter, cut heart or star shaped portions. All this helps to make variety.

Gelatine can also be used for salad. Use a Lemon Jelly recipe or one with tomato (sometimes cook books call this Aspic Jelly) and then put in vegetables exactly as you put in fruit in the recipe below. This makes a delicious salad and also is a nice way to use up small portions of vegetables.

For Lemon Jelly you will need 1 package of granulated gelatine; 1 cupful of sugar; 2 or 3 lemons—enough to make ½ cupful of juice.

For Fruit Gelatine you will need in addition, 1 orange, 2 peaches and some white or seedless grapes. Any other fruit you prefer may be used, but there must be enough to make 1½ cupfuls after it is peeled and diced.

For utensils you will need one jelly mould—a round dish, deep enough to hold three cupfuls will do nicely—a saucepan for heating water, a measuring cup, a wire strainer, a tablespoon, a mixing bowl, a knife and squeezer for the lemons.

Now—hands clean? Aprons on? Here we go!

LEMON JELLY

Dissolve 1 tablespoonful of granulated gelatine in ¼ cupful of cold water.

Let it stand for twenty minutes.

Bring one cupful of water to a boil and pour over the soaked gelatine.

Stir till well dissolved and strain through the wire strainer.

Add ½ cupful of sugar and ½ cupful lemon juice. To get lemon juice, roll the lemons, cut in half and squeeze out the juice into a cup.

Stir gently and pour into the jelly mould.

Set in a cool place and when cold, cover tightly and chill. This will have to stand at least four hours before serving. It may stand over night.

FRUIT GELATINE

Use the Lemon Jelly recipe exactly until the gelatine is in the mould ready to cool. While the gelatine is cooling, peel and dice enough fresh fruit to make 1½ cupfuls. Dice the fruit into neat, even pieces about ⅓ inch square and immediately sprinkle with ½ cupful of powdered sugar so the fruit will not turn brown.

When the gelatine is well cooled, but not cold and set, stir in the fruit very gently, being sure it is well blended through the gelatine.

Then cover tightly and chill.

After you have learned to make gelatine, you will find you can make a great variety of desserts. Try some from Mother's cooking magazine, or from the little book that comes in the box of gelatine. Sometimes the advertisements in the magazines which you find on the library table, have very nice gelatine recipes. This is a time for enterprising cooks to experiment.

DESSERTS—PUDDINGS

OUR third dessert lesson is on dishes that are baked in the oven. You will like baking because it seems so magical—just as though you put dough in the oven and, presto, the oven fairy turns it into something good to eat! But even though it does seem like magic, it's the science of chemistry, too. And there isn't such a thing as "luck." You put in the right things, just as the recipe says, you have the heat right, the length of time right and *then* out comes your beautiful, luscious-smelling food.

By the way, speaking of temperature reminds us that we meant to suggest that you look up oven thermometers. Have you ever seen one? Does your stove have one? I hope you have a thermometer because then you can set it just right. You can be sure you never waste gas and that your food bakes exactly as fast as it should.

Our first pudding is an Apple Pudding. You've cooked apples before, you say? To be sure! Apples are such good food—just the thing for girls and boys and grownups, as well, so cook them often. Fortunately now-a-days we can get apples almost the whole year round, which is lucky.

But this recipe is very different from the apple dishes which we learned to cook earlier in the book. This is a regular pudding, if you please. Be sure to use a good-looking pudding dish to bake it in, for it goes to the table in the dish in which it is baked. A glass or earthenware dish which sets in a silver rack is fine, but if you haven't that, you can use a plain glass or earthen bowl and pin a clean napkin around the sides before you take it to the table.

Cooking apples are best for this pudding if you can get them. This means apples that have not much sugar in their juices. These will get tender in cooking and will make the best pudding. See that you have some dry bread—enough to make two cupfuls of crumbs. A lemon, cupful of sugar, some ground cinnamon and, if you like them, some raisins—the tiny seedless ones are best. Be sure you use a standard brand so that they are perfectly fresh.

Get out a rather flat baking dish and butter it carefully, and while you have the butter out you might measure what you want for the pudding (six tablespoonfuls) and put it on a dish. The supply of butter should be returned to the ice box at once, and it should never be allowed to remain in a warm kitchen. Butter is a very delicately flavored food and should always be kept in a cool place and away from other foods.

Now, with all this done, we are ready for work.

APPLE PUDDING

Wash, peel, core and cut into small slices enough apples to make 3 cupfuls of sliced fruit.

Prepare 2 cupfuls of dry bread crumbs.

Arrange 1 cupful of apple in the bottom of a buttered baking dish. Sprinkle over this ⅔ cupful of crumbs.

Sprinkle over the crumbs ½ cupful sugar, and ½ teaspoonful ground cinnamon.

Drip over that 2 tablespoonfuls melted butter.

Add another layer of apples (1 cupful), and top it with crumbs, butter, sugar, and cinnamon as before.

Add a third layer, using the last cupful of apple and finishing off the top with the last third of the crumbs, butter, cinnamon, and sugar.

Now over the top drip the juice of one lemon.

This makes a fine flavor, but may be omitted if you prefer.

Notice that you have used 1½ cupfuls of sugar. This makes fairly sweet pudding, but when you make it again you can use half a cupful more or less if this is not exactly to your taste.

Pour 1 cupful of cold water over the whole pudding.

Bake for one hour in a moderate oven.

Serve hot. Left over pudding is very good. It may be served cold and is nice for a school luncheon.

"But you didn't use the raisins!" exclaims one observing young person.

No, we didn't yet, because strictly speaking, they are not needed in the recipe. But in our kitchen, we put raisins in almost everything, as we like them so well. So when we make an apple pudding, we mix 1 cupful of raisins with the 3 cupfuls of apples and get them into the pudding that way.

You may serve the pudding plain or with cream or with a hard sauce.

Cream together:

   3 tablespoonfuls butter

   2 tablespoonfuls cream

   2 cupfuls confectioner's sugar

Add ⅓ teaspoon vanilla flavoring

Beat to a cream

Serve in a small bowl.

While your pudding bakes, wash up the knives and other utensils, and make the kitchen tidy. And then, when you serve it, see if your family doesn't think it the best dish you have made.

CHRISTMAS PUDDING

Into a mixing bowl put 1 cupful sugar

   ½ cupful butter

   2 eggs (both white and yellow parts)

   ½ teaspoonful ground nutmeg

   1 teaspoonful ground cloves

   1½ teaspoonfuls ground cinnamon

   1 tablespoonful cocoa

Mix till creamy and smooth.

Add 1 cupful sour cream (sour milk will do but the pudding will not be quite as rich).

2 cupfuls of flour sifted twice with 1 teaspoonful soda and ½ teaspoonful baking powder. As you add the flour, save out a little—about ¼ cupful. Add all the rest and beat until well blended.

Get ¾ of a cup of nut meats (a smaller quantity can be used) and ¾ of a cup of seedless raisins.

Shake the remaining bit of flour over these and toss till every bit is covered with flour. This method prevents the nuts and raisins from settling to the bottom of the cake.

Add the nuts and raisins and stir gently.

Pour into a well greased cake pan, onto the bottom of which you have fitted a piece of brown paper, well greased. Use a pan, which has a center cone so that your pudding, when done, will have a hole in the center.

Bake for 50 minutes in a moderate oven. Test as you tested muffins to make sure it is well baked.

Remove to a serving dish. Stick a sprig of holly in the center hole, surround with sprigs of holly and serve at once with your favorite sauce.

CHRISTMAS PUDDING SAUCE

Separate the yellows and whites of 3 eggs.

Beat the yellows till thick and then add 6 tablespoonfuls confectioner's sugar. Beat again.

Whip the whites until stiff.

Whip in the mixture of yellows and sugar.

Flavor with 1 teaspoonful vanilla extract.

Serve immediately from a deep bowl.

Of course this pudding can be used at any time of the year.

For a change you can bake it in little paper baking cups; ice the tops with an icing made of 2 cupfuls of confectioner's sugar, 3 tablespoonfuls of cream and 2 tablespoonfuls of butter. These pack well and will make a surprise for a college sister or brother.

P. S. Vera, one of our Canadian cooks, writes to say that she is going to cook her Mother's birthday dinner and, please, what shall she cook? We suggest:

Cream of spinach soup

Mutton chops   Baked potatoes

Muffins   Jam

Orange salad

Apple Pudding   Hard sauce

Vera can make the soup early in the day and reheat it in the double boiler. She can make the pudding first, then put in the potatoes (they take 50 minutes), then the muffins. The hard sauce and the salad can be made ahead of time and put in a cool place.

We know you will have a fine dinner, Vera, and that your Mother will be very proud of your skill

SUNDAY EVENING TEA

SUNDAY evening tea offers the best opportunity for youthful cooks to do their stunts. Father is at home and has plenty of time to enjoy what you make. Mother has been busy all day and will appreciate a vacation. And brothers and sisters may have guests who also like good dishes. So do your best to give them all a treat.

If you have on one of your best dresses or suits, change it before you begin cooking, or else put on a coverall apron. A well-trained cook always works in washable clothing. It seems much daintier as well as more sanitary.

Today's lesson is very important, for you not only make a dish for Sunday Evening Tea but you also learn *two* ways to cook eggs. The first, plain boiled for picnics and the second, a more dressy dish that is good not only for tea, but for luncheon or breakfast as well. So put on your thinking caps and work your hardest.

We are first learning to cook an egg dish. There are several reasons for this choice. Mother always has eggs in the house all the year around. Egg dishes are quickly made, and that is an advantage in Sunday cooking. Then too this creamed egg dish, slightly changed, may be made so many many different ways that learning to cook it is *almost* as good as learning a dozen recipes all at once.

Maybe you happen to be one of the very fortunate children who live in the country. If you are, you can run out to the barn and gather the eggs you will need for this lesson. If there are four in your family, you will need six eggs, for everyone will want a big helping of this good dish you are going to make.

If you live in the city, you must look in the pantry or ice box and see if there are six eggs. If there are, ask Mother if you may use them. If there are not that many eggs, or if she needs them for something else, ask if you may buy some more for your cooking. And before you start for the grocery, tell her you will need flour (just a little), butter, salt, and bread. A good cook always makes sure that she has all supplies before she begins work, you know.

I hope you cooks, who are going to market for eggs will remember the story of Humpty Dumpty —all the king's horses and all the king's men couldn't put Humpty Dumpty together again after he fell down from the wall. We've often wondered who Humpty Dumpty was. He must surely have belonged to the egg family somewhere, for all the king's horses and all the king's men working day and night couldn't put an egg together after it fell down and smashed on the sidewalk. So hold your package carefully and watch your step!

Now for other supplies. Get out a small bowlful of flour, some butter, salt, and bread. Cut four pieces of bread in thin slices ready to toast. If Mother does not like you to use a bread knife, you can use crackers instead of toast. Of course you have many times helped Mother to make toast; or you have watched toast being made. So you know how to use the electric or gas toaster or to toast over open coals (using a long fork) just as grown-ups do. Don't let your toast brown too fast; the slower it toasts, the better it tastes.

Everyone ready? Clean hands and aprons? Then here is the recipe.

CREAMED EGGS ON TOAST

Put 6 eggs in a saucepan with 3 cupfuls of water. Bring to a boil.

Boil briskly for 20 minutes.

Remove from the fire. With a large spoon, lift the eggs one by one from the saucepan and drop them gently into a pan of cold water. (If possible let the cold water run on them for 3 minutes. This will loosen the shells.)

Remove the shells.

This is the end of the recipe for plain boiled eggs. Just wrap each egg in paraffin paper and put in a cool place until you pack the basket. Don't forget salt and pepper. For creamed eggs, go right along with the rest of the recipe.

Cut each egg in quarters, lengthwise. This can be done with a silver knife. Now this much of the recipe can be done any time during the day. But the rest must be cooked in the last half hour before mealtime.

Melt 3 tablespoonfuls of butter in a metal pan. (Do not use enameled ware for this as it might chip.) Melt the butter over a slow fire. While it is melting, measure out 1 cupful of milk (or canned milk diluted according to directions).

Measure 3 tablespoonfuls of flour and very gently and gradually stir it into the melted butter. Don't be worried if it looks lumpy. Stir and stir over a low fire until it cooks smooth.

Very, very slowly, pour in the cupful of milk, stirring the mixture all the while so that the milk cooks into the butter and flour.

When this white sauce is smooth and creamy, add ¾ teaspoonful of salt and the quartered eggs. Put over a very low fire where it can barely simmer while you toast the bread or crackers.

Arrange the toast on a warm platter or on individual plates.

Pour the creamed eggs over the toast.

If you prefer, dip the eggs from the saucepan with a spoon, being sure that you scrape all the good sauce from the pan.

Garnish with cress or parsley and serve at once.

And let me tell you a secret. The cook who can make a fine white sauce for creamed eggs is well on the way to being a good cook. Think how many dishes can be made with white sauce—potatoes, fish, chicken and many vegetables. Aren't you glad you learned it?

EGGS AND MUSHROOMS ON TOAST

This recipe is almost like the one before so watch carefully for changes that are suggested.

While the eggs are boiling wash and peel the tops and chop the stems of enough mushrooms to make 1 cupful.

Melt 2 tablespoonfuls of butter in a saucepan. Put in the mushrooms and let them cook very slowly while you make the white sauce. This should take 15 to 20 minutes.

When the sauce is ready to add the eggs, add the mushrooms also and proceed exactly as for eggs on toast.

CREAMED CHICKEN

Cut up enough cooked chicken to make 1½ cupfuls. Cooked veal may be used for this or white tuna fish. Notice that you can make three different dishes with this one recipe.

Make a white sauce exactly as for Creamed Eggs.

Add the cut-up meat and cook 15 minutes in a double boiler so that the whole will be very hot.

SHRIMP AND CHEESE A LA NEWBURG

Make a white sauce using half the quantity called for in the recipe for Creamed Eggs.

Put this sauce in the top of a double boiler and keep it hot.

Add 1½ cupfuls cheese cut fine and stir gently so that it melts through the sauce.

Add 1 cupful of shrimp (this is the quantity usually sold in a small can)—a little more or a little less does not change the recipe.

Add 1 teaspoonful of chopped sweet pepper.

Cook this mixture 10 minutes to make sure all is hot.

Garnish with parsley and a few shakes of paprika.

Lobster or Crabmeat may be used in this same recipe so you have three possible dishes in one rule.

CHEESE BISCUITS

Make baking-powder biscuits exactly as in the recipe, pages 19, 20, only pat them thin—about ⅓ inch thick.

Put half the biscuits in pans ready for baking.

On the top of each biscuit put ¾ teaspoonful pimento cheese. (It is not necessary to measure the cheese in a spoon each time. Measure twice to see the quantity, and then, with a knife, cut about that same quantity until every biscuit has its top of cheese.)

Put another biscuit on top of the cheese. Set it firmly so it will fit well.

Bake 13 minutes.

MEALS AND LUNCHES ON SHORT NOTICE

WHEN we had the book written this far, Jack, one of our nine-year-old friends, asked to see the part we had written. He looked it over carefully. Then he said in a very disappointed voice, "But you haven't anything about picnics and sudden parties and any of those nice times. You just have regular meals."

"But don't you like regular meals?" we asked in great surprise—for people who knew him thought Jack liked eating at almost any time.

"Oh, yes," he admitted. "But I like picnics better. I'd rather eat by the roadside with Mother and Father and Jane and me cooking dinner than to eat any meal in a dining room. I wish you'd say something about that kind of cooking."

Well, we had this lesson planned before Jack spoke, of course. So all we said was, "Wait and see! You'll be surprised!"

And then, without even saying another word about camp fires and picnics (much as we love them), we go right along with the lesson that we had planned.

This lesson is about things you may use almost any time. For instance, when company comes in unexpectedly on Sunday evening, these things will be good. Or perhaps you and your friends play so hard sometimes that Mother allows you to cook something in the middle of the afternoon. That doesn't happen often, of course, but it does sometimes. Or, maybe you have an impromptu party Saturday and your friends stay for luncheon and you want one more tasty dish to add to the menu— something you can cook quickly. Or you may have a porch picnic—you know the sort of times we mean.

When the guests come, just turn to this chapter and get ideas.

First we're going to make Cheese Delights—Had you guessed? For these you will need bread that is at least one day old and American cheese—that means the regular yellow cheese we all like so well. Sometimes it comes in a big round cheese and the groceryman cuts us a slice shaped like a piece of pie. Sometimes it comes in smaller, brick-shaped cheeses and we buy a neat, square slice. Be sure to get good fresh cheese, not too strong. Then you'll need butter. We can't tell you exactly how much of each of these things you'll need, for we don't know how many sandwiches you want to make. But if you have four or five people to serve, you will want nearly a whole loaf of bread, at least one-half pound of cheese, and one-quarter of a pound of butter. Tell Mother to please let you buy plenty, for Cheese Delights are very good, and if you don't use all the material provided, it will keep till the next day. If your family likes paprika, be sure there is some on hand—a little goes a long way.

You will want a sharp bread knife, a large cookie pan, a pancake turner (for handling the hot Cheese Delights), a bowl for creaming butter, a spoon to use with the bowl, a small knife for cutting cheese, and a silver knife for spreading. A dessert spoon is good for the butter and an ordinary dinner knife is fine for spreading the bread.

Now we have come to the place where younger cooks will have to call for help. If you have never cut bread before, ask Mother if you may try it with her standing close by to show you how. Set the bread sidewise on the cutting board. Steady the

loaf with your left hand and cut down slowly and steadily with your right. A knife is a very useful tool, and as soon as possible every CHILD LIFE Cook must learn how to use it. If you are careful to notice that what you are cutting is steady, and that your left hand is well out of the way of the path of the knife *before* you begin actual cutting, you will find it safe and easy. If Mother thinks you should not do this part of the work yourself, ask her to slice the bread for you, cutting a one-pound loaf into about twenty slices.

After the bread is sliced and piled up nicely, ready to spread, slice the cheese into thin, neat slices. It doesn't matter if they break a little, but keep them as neat as you can. Now for the recipe:

CHEESE DELIGHTS

Cream butter by working it in a bowl until it is soft enough to spread.

Butter slices of bread cut from day-old bread.

On alternate slices of buttered bread, arrange neat, thin slices of cheese.

If you like paprika, shake a dash over the cheese.

Cover the cheese with another slice of bread, buttered side down.

Cut in half, cornerwise.

Lay the sandwiches thus made in a cookie pan.

Put in a hot oven and brown.

Remove from the oven and take from the pan with a pancake turner.

Serve while very hot.

For Sunday evening tea serve Cheese Delights with cocoa or plain milk and everyone will be pleased.

Now let's see! How about that camping party? Campers cannot find anything better for a September picnic than Cheese Delights, and this is the way to plan for them over a camp fire.

Add to your list of needed utensils a wire toaster.

Make the Cheese Delights by the regular rule (except that you leave the sandwiches full size instead of cutting them in half) till you come to the place where the recipe says to put them onto the

cookie pan. Instead, wrap each sandwich in paraffin paper and pack it in your lunch basket.

When the campfire has burned down to good hot coals, arrange about four sandwiches in the wire toaster and toast them slowly over the coals. You must do it slowly so the cheese has time to get hot and to melt. Serve at once. Aren't they the best things you ever ate?

Here's something else nice to know. In September, cold sandwiches don't seem to taste so well as they do in the hot summer time. Try toasting all your sandwiches—jelly, meat, nut—and see if their crisp hotness doesn't somehow go better with autumn parties.

PEANUT TOAST

Cut slices of day-old bread and toast on one side.

Spread the untoasted side with butter and peanut butter. To do this easily, cream together equal parts of plain butter and peanut butter and add a pinch of salt. You can tell about how much to use when you decide how many pieces of toast you intend to make.

Arrange the slices on a shallow pan.

Slip them into the broiling oven and toast until the butter is soft and browning.

Serve piping hot.

This is a delicious toast for a camp fire picnic.

If you make it without a broiling oven, spread the butters (which you can mix together at home and carry in a covered jar) on the toasted side. Then toast the underside over the hot coals. This gives the butter a chance to get hot without slipping down into the fire.

A few chopped nuts—any kind—added to the butter make a nice change if you make these often.

HAM TOAST

For a change use finely chopped ham instead of peanut butter. Cream it with the butter and proceed exactly as before.

SANDWICHES

THINKING of picnics reminded us that we must have a whole lesson on sandwiches. Then whenever we have a chance to go to the woods, we shall know something very good that we can take as our share of the party. And such a time as we have had deciding what is the very nicest thing we can cook for the picnic basket! Of course we might say meat sandwiches as they are always good, But everybody knows how to make them—just bread and butter and meat, so it takes nothing but neatness and practice. And you learned how to cook plain boiled eggs earlier in the book.

By the way, one CHILD LIFE Cook says she makes little individual packages of pepper and salt and wraps them inside the last fold of the paraffin paper around the egg. Don't you think that's a fine scheme?

But we don't want a lesson on something everyone can make. We want something so different that the first minute the picnic people get a taste they will say, "My, but this is good! Who brought it?" And then you can tell your recipe. You know how glad that makes a person feel.

So, after a great deal of thinking, we have decided to make raisin sandwiches.

Now, you must not think that this means putting some raisins between pieces of buttered bread; for it means no such easy thing. Raisin sandwiches are made from a raisin filling that is so good you'll have to whistle all the time it cools if you are to keep yourself from eating it before time for sandwich making begins.

For one pound loaf of bread made into sandwiches (about 20 sandwiches), you will need 1 lemon, ½ cupful of sugar, 1 tablespoonful of cornstarch, 1 cupful of raisins, and butter for spreading the bread. The quantity of butter you need depends on how thickly you spread

it. Oh, yes, be sure to cut the bread into very thin slices. Perhaps you can get someone to do that for you after the raisin filling is made and is cooling. If you do not use all the filling the first day, it can be put into a covered cup or dish and kept in a cool place for a day or two.

Look over your supplies and be sure that you have everything you need. Also get out the food grinder and see that you know how to use it, for you will want to grind the raisins. If Mother thinks you should not use the food grinder, perhaps you can chop the raisins in the chopping bowl.

The girls and boys, who have been cooking from the beginning will know that right here they must wash their hands, clean their finger nails, and put on fresh aprons before they begin to cook.

RAISIN SANDWICHES

Grind or chop fine 1 cupful of raisins.

Grate the rind of 1 lemon.

Press out the juice of this lemon and add it to ¾ cupful of water.

Put the water, juice, grated rind, pinch of salt and ½ cupful of sugar into a saucepan.

Boil for 6 minutes.

While it is boiling, dissolve together 1 tablespoonful of cornstarch and ¼ cupful of water.

Stir this into the boiling mixture and boil slowly stirring constantly for 4 minutes.

Stir in the raisins, ground or chopped, and boil for 1 minute.

Pour into a bowl and set aside to cool.

To make the sandwiches:

Butter one-half the slices of bread with creamed butter. (This means butter that has been slightly warmed and worked with a spoon so it spreads well.)

Spread the other slices with raisin filling; use plenty.

Fit a buttered slice with a raisin slice and trim off crusts.

Wrap the sandwiches in paraffin paper and pack for the picnic.

Sometime when Mother or cook makes pie crust, ask her to let you have the scraps. Then cut the pastry into squares and spread them thickly with the raisin mixture. Bake in a quick oven and eat as soon as cool. These are also delicious for a picnic meal. Or maybe sometime you can make tarts with raisin filling for the inside part.

You see, raisin filling is a very convenient as well as a delicous bit of food. Aren't you glad you have learned how to make it?

NOTES ON SANDWICH MAKING

Many kinds of sandwiches are made by this general method. The variation is in using different kinds of fillings.

Most people use plain white bread for sandwiches. But if you make many, you will want to use some other kinds of bread for a change. For instance, brown bread makes a good jelly sandwich. Graham bread is best for a lettuce sandwich, or, indeed, for any salad sandwich.

For still greater variety, you can sometimes use one slice of white bread and the other of graham bread for the sandwich. This not only looks pretty, but tastes good.

Use mayonnaise or a good cooked salad dressing with salad sandwiches. In this way the bread never gets soggy. *Always* cream the butter before spreading it on the bread.

BAR-LE-DUC FILLING

Into a mixing bowl put 3 tablespoonfuls of cream cheese and ⅓ teaspoonful salt

3 tablespoonfuls currant jelly (or grape jelly)

With a fork, mix until well blended.

Notice that no dressing is used in this.

Spread filling on brown or graham bread.

DATE AND NUT FILLING

Wash and seed enough dates to make ¾ cupful.

Pick over enough nut meats to make ½ cupful.

Put both ingredients through grinder, using the coarse cutter.

Mix with enough mayonnaise to make a smooth-spreading paste.

Use as in making Raisin Sandwiches.

HAM AND EGG FILLING

Boil 3 eggs for 20 minutes.

Plunge them into cold water and remove shells.

Measure about ½ cupful of cooked ham. This may be end bits from a baked ham, it may be scraps from a slice of broiled or fried ham or it may be slices of broiled ham bought just for this use. The quantity should be a little more in bulk than the three eggs.

Put eggs and ham through the grinder together, using a coarse cutter.

Mix with mayonnaise until soft enough to spread.

PEANUT SANDWICHES

Spread alternate slices of thinly cut bread with peanut butter and with a tart jelly such as grape or currant or plum.

Press slices together and cut in triangles.

This sandwich is excellent when made with toasted bread or in a three layer sandwich of toast, one layer spread with peanut butter, one with jelly and one with salad dressing and lettuce.

COOKIES AND SIMPLE CAKES

"THAT'S my favorite!" exclaimed one Child Life cook, as she glanced at the top of this page. Well, to be sure! Cookies are favorites with everyone and that's why it is so very important that we learn to make them well. Cookies come in so handy, don't they? They taste fine in a school lunch box. Nothing is better than cocoa and cookies for a luncheon dessert, or fruit and cookies for dinner. And as for parties and picnics, and after swimming lunches and such—well, a person just has to have cookies. That's all there is to it! So we are going to make several kinds, all very good. And we are going to learn to make all of them so easily and so well that cookie-making will be no trouble at all.

It might be a good thing to remind ourselves right here about some things we never intend to forget. Cookie making means baking in the oven, and that means paying very close attention from start to finish. It will never do to put the cookies in the oven and then run out and play. Of course the heat of the oven does the real work of baking, but the cook has to stay right on the job to make sure the heat is hot enough—and no more; that the cookies get a beautiful brown— and no more; and that they are taken out at exactly the right minute.

Also, cookie-making is apt to be muss-making in the kitchen and if a young cook is not very careful, she or he will become most unpopular in a short time. So spread a clean paper on the floor before beginning work; be dainty as you can all along and clean up every bit of the muss—dishes, utensils, table and sink—before you leave the kitchen. If you manage well, you can do all this while the last cookies are baking, and with the cookies all luscious smelling and the kitchen clean, you can be sure you did a good job and will be allowed to work again.

We are going to make Oatmeal Cookies first because they can be dropped from a spoon to the baking pan—a process that is more simple than rolling out dough. We will learn that later. Another reason why we choose this recipe is because it is so very good—you'll find your cookies very popular winter or summer.

Look in the pantry and see if Mother has these materials on hand: oatmeal, raisins, sugar, flour, eggs, soda, milk (sweet, sour, or canned, it doesn't matter which), shortening, ground cinnamon and salt. You can look ahead to see how much of each article will be needed, and if necessary go to the grocery for supplies. If you find some nuts and a little orange marmalade, so much the better, but these are not really necessary. Isn't it fun to be making something that takes "sugar and spice and everything nice"?

For utensils you will need a mixing bowl, a measuring cup, a mixing spoon, a tablespoon, a teaspoon, a saucer, a pancake turner and a cookie pan—two pans are even better than one. Now with all your materials and utensils together, we can begin work.

OATMEAL COOKIES

Measure 2 cupfuls of oatmeal (any standard brand.)
3 cupfuls sifted flour.
1 cupful sugar
into a mixing bowl and gently mix them together.

Make a little hollow in the center and into this put:

2 eggs. Crack the shell sharply against the side of the table, insert your thumb, push the two halves of shell apart and drop the egg into a saucer, then from that into mixing bowl.

1 cupful of shortening. This may be butter or vegetable oil. Or you may take ½ cupful of meat drippings (the fat from sausage or bacon is fine) and ½ cupful of any of the shortenings mentioned.

> **¾ teaspoonful soda dissolved in**
> **4 tablespoonfuls milk**
> **½ tablespoonful salt**
> **1 heaping teaspoonful ground cinnamon.**

Then if you have them and like the flavor, add

½ cupful nut meats crushed fine and

1 tablespoonful orange marmalade. These are not really necessary.

Mix and blend all these ingredients together until you have a smooth mass.

Oil the cookie pan by rubbing fat or vegetable oil over it with a bit of soft white paper.

Drop the dough in lumps the size of a small egg and arrange in nice even rows. This recipe makes from 48 to 60 cookies, depending upon the size.

Bake in a moderate oven until the cookies are a tempting brown color. This will take about 20 minutes.

Remove from the pan while hot, using the pancake turner and placing the cookies on a towel or a cake rack. **When cool, pack in a jar** or tin box.

Wash and put away all utensils while the last batch of cookies bake.

What's that? You're going to eat all the cookies that break while being taken from the pan? But we didn't break any—we were just that careful! So suppose we fix a plateful of beautiful, perfect cookies and pass them to our family. Isn't cooking fun?

SAND TARTS

This is an old fashioned recipe—about 200 years old—but after you have learned to make the tarts, you will think there isn't anything better or more fun.

Into a **mixing bowl put ½ pound of granulated sugar** (1 cup)

> **½ pound flour (2 cups)**
> **2 eggs**
> **¼ pound butter (½ cup)**
> **1 teaspoonful flavoring.**

With spotlessly clean fingers, rub and rub and rub these four ingredients together until you have a smooth soft dough. Some cooks take two knives and cut the mixture until it is a smooth dough but fingers are better and quicker we think.

When it is a smooth, even mass, divide it into four balls. Remove all the dough from your fingers and wash your hands.

Flour the cookie board and roll out one of the dough balls until it is very thin. It must be just as thin as you can roll it and make it stay together firmly.

Cut the cookies (or tarts as they used to be called) with cookie cutters. With a pancake turner or a broad spatula remove them from the board to the baking pan.

After trimming the cookies, bake in a moderate oven until a pretty, light brown.

Remove from the pan with a spatula to a wire rack.

When cool, pack in a tin box or stone jar. These cookies will keep for weeks—provided you can keep your family from eating them up—we can't!

Trimming the cookies. This is jolly fun so think up all the different ways you can; here are some to start with:

1. Put a white of an egg in a sauce dish and with dainty fingers, dip two fingers in the egg and rub over the top of a cookie. This makes a pretty glaze when the cookie is baked.

2. Mix together 2 tablespoonfuls of sugar and 1 teaspoonful of ground cinnamon. Next, put this into a salt shaker and shake the mixture over the cookie.

3. With a clean, new paint brush—a tiny one such as you use for watercolor paints—put melted sweet chocolate on the cookie in designs. This is nice for an anniversary or birthday party and you can use numbers or initials.

4. Candied cherries, cut in half so they will lay flat, and nut meats, make a nice trimming.

Decide on four or fewer ways of trimming and then do one ball of dough each way. Do not try too many styles at one baking as it will take too long, and will be confusing.

Have at least two panfuls of cookies ready and trimmed before you start baking as these cookies brown quickly and must be carefully watched.

SWEETMEATS

ONCE upon a time there was a little girl—oh, about as old as you are maybe—and she cooked a very good dinner all by herself. Think of that! She cooked meat and potatoes and vegetables, and soup of course. That came first. And she cooked dessert and made a good salad and everything was just as good as you could possibly imagine food could be. And her little brother cooked, too, for he was a very, *very* bright boy and he knew perfectly well that if he wanted to go camping and have house parties and all such fun, he'd better learn how to cook a meal by himself.

And then, after all that, they wanted to cook some more! Think of that! They wanted to cook some food that wasn't just regular "meal-eating" food but was sort of "extra-like." This food is for parties and Christmas time and boxes to send to folks away and such things.

Now you mustn't think that these two nice people ate candy between meals and pieced so that they couldn't enjoy regular food. Dear me, no! We wouldn't put that kind of a person in our nice cook book, you may be sure. Just *because* they were such good cooks and so wise about their eating, we want to put in this chapter on extra goodies that we know every Child Life cook will love to make. So we put our thinking caps on—right on top of our pretty white cook's cap—and we thought up all the good things you are going to make in a minute.

But before we get to cooking perhaps it would be fun to talk a minute about holiday times in general. When Thanksgiving or Christmas or a birthday time comes around, there is so much going on in the kitchen that there is hardly a corner where a small cook can work. Haven't you noticed that? Everyone is so busy

roasting turkey or making pies or getting great pans of vegetables on to cook that there isn't any place left in which to work. Don't be discouraged about that for there is much you can do to help that isn't actually cooking. A Child Life cook can help before hand by cleaning silver and sorting napkins and helping with decorations, to say nothing of errands and a dozen other ways of helping. And here's a secret. If you help before hand so that mother and cook know you are truly interested, you are much more likely to be allowed to help on the final big day—oh, much!

Another point, all the recipes in this chapter are for goodies that can be made the day before and then packed in a tin box for safe keeping. It's much wiser to do your work before the final big day comes around and then you can enjoy the comfortable feeling of being ready ahead of time. Every one of our recipes, too, is fine for things to send in a box. So if you want to send a surprise to brother or sister off at college or to grandmother on her birthday, this is the chapter you want to study.

Our first recipe is for Candied Orange Peel. We choose this because it is so unusual and so pretty and also because it is wholesome to eat. After you have learned to make it you will want to make a batch very often and keep it on hand in a tightly covered tin box. Father will like a bit with his after dinner coffee; Mother will serve it with afternoon tea, and some time you will take a whole boxful of it to school when your room has a party.

For making Candied Orange Peel you will need the rind from three thin-skinned oranges (any sort of orange will do, but the thin-skinned ones are finer

flavor and rather more tasty for this use) and two cupfuls of sugar. If you have halves of oranges for breakfast, save the rind, wash, drain and use those. If you don't have oranges that morning, you can cut the three oranges in half, crosswise, loosen the pulp with a sharp knife, remove with a tin spoon and set it aside for Mother or cook to use for salad at dinner time. But likely, if you ask Mother the night before, she will plan to have oranges for breakfast and then the empty rinds will be cut all ready for you to use. You may wish to make more candied peel than this one recipe; if so, start over again with a second set of three oranges. That will be better than to attempt to make too much all at once.

For utensils you will need a small and a large saucepan, a large plate, a fork, a tin or other sharp-edged spoon and some sheets of paraffin paper.

RECIPE FOR CANDIED ORANGE PEEL

Put a quart of water into a saucepan and bring to a brisk boil.

Drop into this the six halves of orange peel and cook for five minutes.

With your fork, turn the rinds other side up and cook for five minutes more. (If you have had to use a thick-skinned orange, cook it three minutes longer.)

Remove the pan from the stove. Take the rinds from the pan and plunge quickly into cold water to cool.

With your tin spoon remove all the pithy white portion from the inside of the rinds. Do this very carefully as the white part is bitter and even a little will spoil your product.

Split open each rind and, laying it flat on the table, cut it into tiny strips. Try to have the strips uniform size and about 2 to 2½ inches long and ⅜ of an inch wide.

Into the small saucepan put 1 cupful of granulated sugar and ⅓ cupful of water. Dissolve and bring to a boil.

Drop in one-half of the cut rinds. With your fork, spread the pieces through the syrup.

Cook at a simmer for 15 minutes.

While these are cooking, spread ½ cupful of granulated sugar on a plate and put a sheet of paraffin paper on the table close by.

At the end of 15 minutes, remove the strips of rind from the saucepan and roll in the sugar. Be sure that each piece is well covered. While you are doing this, the pan of syrup should be set away from the stove so the syrup will not boil too long.

Repeat the cooking and sugaring for the rest of the cut peeling, using the same syrup.

As soon as the strips are sugared, arrange neatly on the paper. When cool they are ready for use.

Grapefruit peeling may be prepared the same way and makes a nice color variety but extra care must be taken in removing the white portion.

Our second recipe is for stuffed Dates. These are good any time of year that dates are on the market —which means any time but summer.

For this you will want two pounds of dates, one cupful of nut meats and a cupful of granulated sugar. Be sure to tell Mother about this several days ahead so she can get your supplies along with her other ordering. Then it would be a good idea for you to look up some nice candy boxes and some paraffin paper. Dates can be prepared ahead of time if they are well packed and put away.

Especial care must be taken when making this or similar recipes to be sure your hands and nails are spotlessly clean. A good cook is always dainty as well as skillful so that the product is appetizing and pretty and good tasting.

Utensils needed are a pan to use while washing the dates, a strainer in which to drain them, a large plate, on which the sugar is put and on which the dates are rolled, and a small knife to slit the date when you remove the seed.

As your hands will get a little sticky, better have a clean towel handy in case you are interrupted, and put paper on the floor to catch any stray sugar. We hope you will be so tidy that not one speck of sugar will be spilled, but just the same, it's not much trouble to spread down a paper and then we are sure of making no muss.

Now for the recipe:

STUFFED DATES

Wash and pick over 2 pounds of dates.

Drain carefully.

Remove seeds. To do this, make a slit in the side of the date; pry out the seed. Be sure to keep the pretty, natural shape of the date.

Fill the place left by the seed with a piece of nut. English walnuts are about the best for this though pecans or any other nut may be used. For each date use ¼ of an English walnut or ½ of a pecan. For variety, fill a few dates with peanut butter moulded into the shape of a date seed.

Form the date into shape and roll in granulated sugar.

Arrange in candy dishes or pack between paraffin paper in candy boxes—tin ones are best.

Figs can be stuffed too. Wash and drain. Press open until you have the round shape as the fig grows. Then stuff with peanut butter or soft creamy cheese. Cut into slices or into four even parts.

NUTTED PRUNES

Wash one pound of fine prunes in three changes of warm water.

Cover with 3 cupfuls of cold water and let stand for 24 hours. Cover tightly. If you wash the prunes and start them soaking after school one afternoon, they will be ready to finish the afternoon of the next day.

Drain off any extra water left at the end of 24 hours. This juice is good for a pudding sauce, so ask Mother if it cannot be used.

With a sharp knife slit each prune and remove the seed. Be very careful not to spoil the shape of the prune.

Put half a nut meat into the prune in place of the pit you removed.

Close the prune and fit it back into natural shape.

Roll in granulated sugar as you did the stuffed dates and pack in tin boxes.

PEANUT PRUNES

Prepare as above, only put a small roll of peanut butter in place of the nut meat.

CHOCOLATE ALMONDS

For this you will need one cake of sweet chocolate (the size usually sold for ten cents will be correct) and 1 cupful of blanched almonds. 'Blanched' means that the nuts, after removal from the shells have been scalded and the brown skin removed. You can buy the nuts blanched or you can blanch them yourself as you prefer.

Put the sweet chocolate in the top of the double boiler and, with plenty of boiling water underneath, melt until it is soft and creamy.

Add ½ teaspoonful vanilla flavoring.

Drop in ⅓ cupful of almonds.

With a fork toss around in the melted chocolate until every nut is covered.

Remove a few at a time, letting the extra chocolate drip off into the double boiler.

Arrange neatly on paraffin paper. Work quickly and arrange the nuts in neat rows, each nut separately. The chocolate will harden quickly.

Do the rest

of the nuts, ⅓ cupful at a time.

When entirely cool and dry, remove from the paper and pack in boxes.

Candied cherries, nuts of any kind and raisins may be covered with chocolate by this same method.

The amount of chocolate you use depends on how thick a covering you want. If you use up one piece, melt more.

FRUIT BALLS

Wash and look over ½ pound figs, ½ pound dates, ½ pound raisins, ½ pound shelled nuts.

Remove all stems, seeds and imperfections.

Put through a grinder using a little of each of the four products at a time so that the ground material will be well mixed.

Put through the grinder a second time to make sure it is well mixed and cut fine. Use the next to the finest cutter for this work. If you have no grinder or think best not to use one, the fruit and nuts can be chopped. Work until they are cut fine and are well blended.

Mold into balls the size of a large marble.

Roll in granulated sugar as you did stuffed dates.

If you want a small amount, use half of the above quantities. But these balls keep well when packed in tin and are nice to have on hand so most cooks prefer to make 2 pounds at a time.

SCHOOL PARTIES

ONE of the most interesting ways to use a knowledge of cooking is to help give a school party. Very likely your class will wish to have several parties during the year, and any girl, or any boy for that matter, who knows how to cook and how to plan refreshments is sure to be a popular person. Of course anyone can think up good things to eat; it is not necessary to know about cooking for that. But only the person who is informed about foods and their preparation can decide which foods are best for serving large groups of people, and which can best be prepared to serve at school. Since all our Child Life cooks go to school, and all schools have parties, this seems to be a most important chapter in our cook book, and we hope that it will be used many, many times.

The first question any refreshment committee asks when it meets to plan for a party is, "What shall we have to eat?" And it is quite right that a decision about the menu should be made first, for plans for serving and for paying the cost of the food cannot be completed until the committee knows what food it is going to set before its guests.

You may propose any one of the following menus:

Doughnuts and Apples
Pop Corn and Homemade Taffy
Apples and Pop Corn
Lemonade and Cookies
Sandwiches and Milk
Cookies and Cocoa
Tea and Wafers or Sandwiches

All of the foods in these combinations are good to eat, fairly easy to serve, and not very expensive.

Perhaps your committee will ask next, "If all these menus are so good, how shall we decide which one to use?" That's a fair question.

You will then consider the equipment for serving and cooking which you have at your schoolhouse and may use, and also the amount of money you will be allowed to spend. Both of these considerations will help you in making a decision as to what to serve.

The first three menus suggested will need neither cooking nor dishes at the schoolhouse. They may be prepared entirely at some person's home. Or, if a large number are to be served and you wish to divide up the labor, the foods may be prepared at two or three different homes, and then carried to school in baskets or pasteboard cartons from which they can be served. You will, to be sure, give each guest a paper napkin, but that is all that will be needed. So if there is no kitchenette in your school building and if you have no supply of dishes, you will be wise if you choose one of the first menus or something very similar.

But if your school equipment includes a stove and kettles as well as cups and plates, and if you are allowed to use them for a class party, you have a much larger range of choice and can use any of the menus suggested. Perhaps even though you have no dishes at school you may have money enough to buy paper cups and plates for the party. In that case your committee can prepare sandwiches or cookies at home and serve milk or lemonade in paper cups. This is an excellent plan and has the additional advantage of making very little labor in the clearing up after the party. It is much easier for girls and boys to collect paper cups and plates and dispose of them than it is to wash and wipe dishes, count them and stack them neatly in the cupboards.

Paper cups will do beautifully for cold beverages, but if you want a hot drink you must have real cups, and with them real plates. And we must admit that sometimes in winter a hot drink is worth all the trouble it causes, for it helps so much toward the success of a party. Tea and cookies or wafers are particularly acceptable when mothers are being entertained, so it is well to keep that fact in mind when you are planning the entertainment schedule for the year.

Sometimes you may wish to give a more elaborate party; then you will surely want to have ice cream and cake. Nothing is more partyish than that menu. Have the caterer freeze the ice cream in individual molds—not those expensive, fancy molds used for formal parties, but small-sized "lily" cups which he can purchase in lots of a hundred. If he cannot conveniently use those, he may freeze the cream in bricks, slice it, and wrap each slice in paraffin paper before he delivers it at the school. Ice cream thus packed in cups or cut in slices and wrapped is easily served at school. Never attempt to serve ice cream from the can, in bulk, as it is likely to be a very messy and unsatisfactory bit of business.

In case you serve little cakes instead of cookies with the ice cream, bake them in paper baking cups, ice the tops, and bring them to school without removing them from the cups. In this way they will keep fresh and unbroken and will be very easy to serve. The Christmas pudding recipe in the chapter on puddings is a good one to use, as is any other simple cake recipe.

If you decide to serve doughnuts and apples, plan to buy the doughnuts or ask some one to contribute them. Doughnuts are rather too difficult for youthful cooks to attempt, but very satisfactory ones can be purchased almost anywhere. In selecting apples, choose small, even-sized ones and wash and polish them well before bringing them to the party.

Have your serving committee meet before the party; they can fold the napkins and place one on each plate, then arrange the plates in neat piles for serving. If you need teaspoons, have the correct number counted out and arranged on trays in advance. Be sure to serve loaf sugar with cocoa, as guests may wish to add sugar. For tea, have ready sugar, lemon, and cream (or milk). The lemon should be cut in very thin slices as shortly before serving time as possible. These "trimmings" should be passed immediately after the tea is served, so that there may be no tedious waiting.

The successful committee always plans all details of the party ahead of time. Some members may take charge of the supplies, others of the serving table, and still others of the actual passing of food. Another group should act as hosts and hostesses, going around among the guests and making sure that all are well served, and that no strangers are left to eat alone. Sometimes it is a good idea for the refreshment committee or the class president to appoint subcommittees to attend to each of these various duties. These committees should consist of not more than three to five students each—just enough to divide up the work, and not enough to cause confusion.

Now that we have talked about all these general matters we may study recipes. Our favorite menu is lemonade and cookies, so we shall learn a recipe for that one first.

LEMONADE FOR A SCHOOL PARTY

Estimate the number of guests to be served. One lemon, one tablespoonful of sugar, and one pint of water will serve three persons.

Divide the number of guests you expect to serve by three and you will have the number of lemons, the tablespoonfuls of sugar, and the amount of water needed. To be sure it is wise and hospitable to provide a little more than one serving to a person, but you can estimate the extra amount you will wish to have on hand and add that to the exact amounts required for one serving for each person.

As sugar is bothersome to count by spoonfuls, refer to the table on the inside cover of this book and figure how many cupfuls you will need. See how useful arithmetic can be? One could hardly give a party without it.

Perhaps it will be wise to measure the cups or glasses you intend to use at the party. Not all hold the same amount, although usually one is safe in counting three to the pint, since the cup or glass cannot, of course, be filled to overflowing.

Method

Extract the juice from the lemons.

Dissolve the sugar in the juice.

Pour into tightly closed glass jars for carrying to school.

If there is a kitchenette at school you may be allowed to make your preparations there, but it is quite as easy and pleasant to do it at home and bring the juice all ready for the addition of water and ice just before serving. Divide up the work and be sure, oh, very sure, that the kitchen in which you work is left neat and tidy—else you may not be welcome a second time.

Mix the juice and sugar with the measured amount of water. For this work you will need a large bowl or kettle, and a ladle for serving.

Add ice enough to chill.

Let stand a few minutes and then serve. Use individual glasses or cups which may be passed on trays. Or serve from a large punch bowl placed on an attractively decorated table.

COCOA FOR A LARGE PARTY

Measure the cups you plan to use and figure the number of persons you can serve from one pint.

Estimate the number of guests expected; divide by the number one pint of cocoa will serve, and make that many times one pint of cocoa. This method of figuring is called "using the pint unit in planning" and is an accurate and easy way of computing the correct amount of supplies needed.

METHOD FOR MAKING ONE PINT OF COCOA

Mix together
  2 teaspoonfuls sugar (beet or cane sugar)
  2 teaspoonfuls cocoa.
Dissolve in ½ cupful of water.
Put ½ cupful of water on to boil and when hot add the dissolved sugar and cocoa.
Boil for 1 minute and then add 1 cupful of milk. Stir carefully while adding the milk to make sure there are no lumps.
Bring to boiling temperature but do not actually boil. The instant boiling begins, remove the kettle from the fire. This method avoids the danger of scorching and also prevents the formation of the troublesome skum on the top of the cocoa.
Serve at once, using a marshmallow as a garnish for each cupful. Whipped cream is also a delicious garnish—use 1 teaspoonful per cup—but it is more expensive and rather more difficult to manage if your party is a large one.
Some people prefer a richer cocoa than this recipe makes. If you wish, you may use half the amount of water called for and for the second half substitute an equal amount of milk. Thus for each pint of cocoa you would use ½ cupful of water and 1½ cupfuls of milk.

TEA FOR A LARGE PARTY

Measure the amount of water needed to serve your guests, and bring the water to a boil.
Allow 1 teaspoonful of tea for each five cupfuls to be made. For this use a black tea, probably Orange Pekoe of a standard brand, is the best.
Make tiny bags of cheesecloth or old linen and tie up the tea, allowing about three teaspoonfuls to each bag. Tie the bags loosely, for the tea will swell when it is wet.
When the water is just ready to boil, drop in the tea bags, remove the kettle from the fire and let stand for five minutes. Then serve.

The secret of good tea is that it shall be freshly made of freshly boiled water, so watch the clock carefully and have the tea ready just on the dot—not a minute ahead of the time it is to be served.
Any of the cookie recipes given in this book would be very acceptable at a school party, but this is our favorite, as it is both good and easy to make.

OLD-FASHIONED DROPPED COOKIES

Into a mixing bowl put
  1 cupful of sugar
  ½ cupful vegetable oil, margarine, or other fat
  ½ teaspoonful ground nutmeg
  ½ teaspoonful ground cinnamon
  2 eggs (both whites and yellows)
Beat till smooth, then add
  1 cupful buttermilk or sour milk
  2 cupfuls of flour into which has been sifted
    1 teaspoonful of soda
    1 teaspoonful of salt
Beat till smooth and then add
  1 cupful of raisins
  1 cupful of nut meats (broken fine). Sprinkle the raisins and nuts with ½ cupful of flour before adding them to the dough.
Beat gently till well blended and then drop by spoonfuls onto buttered cookie tins. NOTE: Some brands of flour thicken more easily than others, so it is impossible to tell for all kinds exactly how much should be used. On the average the 2½ cupfuls called for in the recipe will be just right. If the dough seems "runny" as you drop it from the spoon, add ¼ cupful more of flour and it will be better.
Bake in a moderate oven (400°) till brown. This will take from 12 to 15 minutes.
Lift the cookies from the pan with a cake turner and place them on a wire rack till cool. Then pack in a box lined with paraffin paper.
This recipe will make from 40 to 60 cookies, according to the size. Bake a trial panful of, say, four cookies to see which size you like best and then make the rest all exactly the same size. The finished cookie will be a little larger than the pile of dough, as it will spread in baking.
For variety sometimes omit either the raisins or the nuts, or use chopped peanuts instead of pecans or walnuts. These changes will give the cookies a different flavor.

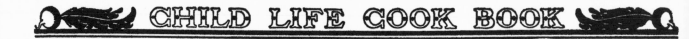
MENUS

BREAKFAST
Orange Juice
Uncooked Rice Cereal and Milk
Scrambled Eggs   Buttered Toast (whole wheat)
Coffee or Milk

Cooked Figs
Cream of Wheat with Milk
Grilled Tomatoes   Toast with Jam
Coffee or Milk

Sliced Peaches (fresh or cooked)
Bran Cereal with Cream
Omelet   French Toast with Jelly
Coffee or Milk

Halves of Grapefruit
Oatmeal with Milk and Honey
Grilled Bacon   Buttered Toast
Coffee or Milk

Sliced Oranges
Uncooked Corn Cereal with Milk
Sausages   Waffles with Syrup
Coffee or Milk

Halves of Melon or Oranges
Whole Wheat Cereal (cooked) with
Milk and Maple Sugar
Grilled Ham   Griddle Cakes
Coffee or Milk

Every breakfast menu should include:
Fruit (cooked or raw)
Cereal with Milk or Cream
A Small Helping of Protein such as
Eggs, Bacon, Ham, or Fish
and some form of
Bread, if desired

LUNCHEON OR SUPPER
Stuffed Tomato Salad
Brown Bread and Butter   Peach Jam
Raspberry Shortcake with Whipped Cream
Milk

Cream of Spinach Soup   Crackers
Fresh Radishes or Celery
Baked Eggs   Brown Bread
Baked Pears with Ginger Sauce

Carrots with Peas
Creamed Potatoes
Gingerbread   Apple Sauce
Raisins on Stems   Cocoa

Lamb Chops   Fresh Asparagus
Lettuce Salad   Whole Wheat Bread
Milk or Cocoa

Asparagus Soup   Crackers
Cheese Omelet   Lettuce Salad
Nut Bread   Conserve
Strawberry Tarts

Peanut Butter Soup   Wafers
Orange Salad   Bread and Butter
Baked Custard

DINNER
Vegetable Soup   Crackers
Corned Beef Hash   Baked Squash
Cabbage Salad   Bran Muffins
Jam
Apple Pudding with Hard Sauce
Coffee or Milk

Cream of Tomato Soup   Salted Wafers
Steak   French Fried Potatoes
Spinach with Mushroom Sauce
Endive Salad   Bread-and-Butter Sandwiches, rolled
After-Dinner Coffee

Cream of Spinach Soup   Toast
Macaroni with Cheese and Tomato
Fresh Green Beans
Bran Muffins   Peach Jam
Grapefruit and Prune Salad
Buttered Wafers
Ambrosia   Little Cakes

Clear Bean Soup   Crackers
Baked Beef Tongue with Vegetables
Escalloped Potatoes
Bread and Butter   Apple Jam
Pear and Nut Salad
Pudding Cake
Tea

Sliced Cold Meat   Delmonico Potatoes
Corn on the Cob   Endive Salad
Berries with Cream   Cookies
Iced Tea with Mint

Clear Tomato Soup   Toasted Wafers
Meat Loaf   Roasted Potatoes
Cauliflower with Cheese Sauce
Whole Wheat Bread   Jelly
Orange Salad with Sweet Wafers
Coffee or Milk

Vegetable Soup   Salt Crackers
Beefsteak Balls with Tomato Sauce
Baked Potatoes   Carrots
Muffins   Conserve
Grapefruit Salad, Cheese Wafers

Cream of Corn Soup   Crackers
Veal Chops   Stuffed Baked Potatoes
Buttered Carrots
Tomato and Lettuce Salad
Cheese Sticks
Baked Custard

MENUS FOR SPECIAL OCCASIONS

A Sunday Tea (midsummer)
Shrimp Salad   Thin Bread-and-Butter Sandwiches
Olives   Pickled Beets   Nuts
Individual Cakes   Fruit Punch

An Autumn Picnic
Broiled Steak   Baked Potatoes
Stuffed Tomato Salad
Sandwiches of Ham, Cheese, Jelly
Peaches   Cookies
Marshmallows for Toasting

A Fourth of July Picnic Dinner

Meat Loaf   Potato Salad
Ham-and-Pickle Sandwiches
Nut-Bread Sandwiches
Stuffed Olives   Fresh Radishes
Chocolate Cake   Raisin Cookies
Ice Cream (or fruit)
Iced Tea with Lemon Slices

A Birthday Dinner

Clear Vegetable Soup
Roast Leg of Lamb   Mint Sauce
Browned Potatoes   Peas
Spiced Crab Apples
Fruit Salad in Orange Baskets
Toasted Bread Strips
Ice Cream Served on Squares of Sponge Cake
and Topped with Fruit Sauce
Demi-tasse Coffee

MEMORANDUM

RECIPES

RECIPES

THE INDEX

THE INDEX